P9-EAX-547

MOVING TO ARIZONA

The Complete Arizona Answer Book

By

Dorothy Tegeler

Fourth Edition

Gem Guides Book Co.

315 CLOVERLEAF DRIVE, SUITE F
BALDWIN PARK, CA 91706

Published by:
Gem Guides Books Company
315 Cloverleaf Dr., Suite F
Baldwin Park, CA 91706

Copyright © 1999 Gem Guides Book Company
Reprinted 2004

Cover Photo: Debs Metzong
Cover Design: Scott Roberts

Printed and bound in the United States of America. All rights reserved. No part of this book may be reproduced in any form or by any electronic means including storage and retrieval systems without permission in writing from the publisher.

ISBN: 1-889786-02-0

Library of Congress Catalog Card Number: 99-73308

CONTENTS

ACKNOWLEDGMENTS

This book bears the name of a single author, but without the cooperation of hundreds of others, it would not be possible. I would like to recognize the many contributors who have helped with this effort, only a few of whom I can mention here.

Special thanks to all the employees of state and local government offices who were never too busy to check on a fact or supply the latest brochure. State agencies such as the Arizona Department of Commerce, Arizona Office of Tourism, Arizona Highways and Arizona Department of Economic Security have been wonderful resources as have many others. Local chambers of commerce are often the best resource for specific details about a particular community. The city, county and state librarians have been very helpful at finding "one more place to check."

Only my family can truly picture the piles of paper that stack up as research is underway, even in an electronic age. A big thank you to my husband, Joe Shryock, for tiptoeing around the office clutter for months without losing patience. A special salute to my little Sheltie, Sady, who sat at my feet for the last 14 years silently supporting my writing efforts and, during this revision, finally gave up her watch. Thanks to a special group of young adults for being there for me–Paul, Laura, and the more recent additions, Kacee, Jeff and Saul.

The editorial staff at Gem Guides deserves recognition for their work in polishing and packaging these words so that they come to you better than they left my desk. A special thanks to Debs Metzong for taking such beautiful pictures of Arizona. I take great pleasure in having them grace the covers of these books.

INTRODUCTION

If you have just moved to Arizona, are about to move or are dreaming of the day when you can move to the Grand Canyon State, this book is for you. *Moving to Arizona* is the Arizona "Answer Book," written especially for the newcomer, with the goal of taking the trauma out of relocating.

This book addresses the immediate concerns of the newcomer—finding housing, a new job, good schools, and a new doctor. You'll find answers to questions about starting a business, getting licensed, registered or certified, as well as finding community and government resources. Relevant state laws are explained. Special health and safety precautions to protect you while enjoying Arizona are discussed.

This book does refer to specific laws, however, it should not be considered as a source for legal information, but a layman's guide to general information. For specific information consult the Arizona Revised Statutes, an attorney or the responsible government agency. Laws and regulations change frequently, do not rely on this book as your final source of information.

You'll find information about the metropolitan Phoenix and Tucson areas—the state's major population centers and a capsule-size history of the state. Not enough to bore you, just enough to whet your appetite.

To help you enjoy your new home state there's a brief introduction to some of the world's most tempting recreational activities. Millions of visitors come to explore the state and to bask in Arizona sunshine each year. Names, addresses and phone numbers are included wherever they might be of help. Please keep in mind that in a state that's growing as fast as Arizona, many agencies outgrow their facilities and relocate. As telephone numbers and area codes are changing frequently, we recommend that you contact the Arizona information operators if you encounter any problems. Many state agencies and businesses also maintain Internet sites. Use your search engines to locate these sites. Since websites seem to change even more frequently than phone numbers in most case they have not been listed here. Some tables and statistics have been updated for this printing. If you discover a change since we went to press, we would appreciate a note sent to the author in care of:

Gem Guides Book Co.
315 Cloverleaf Dr., Suite F
Baldwin Park, CA 91706

We'll be sure to note the change in the next edition.

ARIZONA

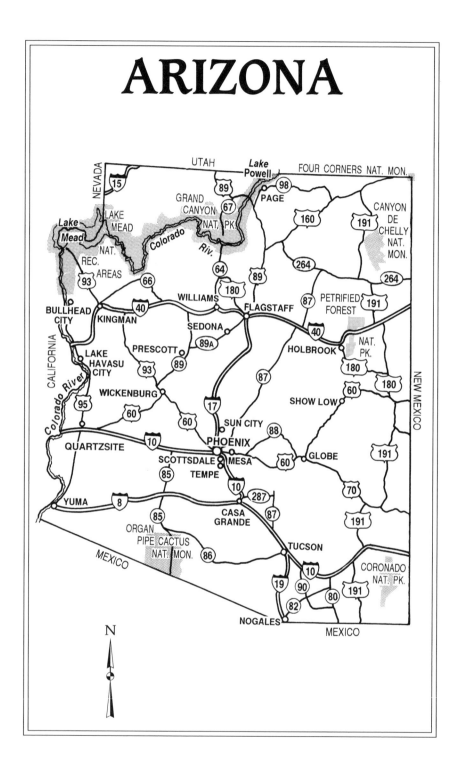

Chapter 1
ARIZONA ON THE GROW

While still a bit reminiscent of the Wild West, Arizona is a state with major urban centers. Phoenix is the nation's 6th largest city and Tucson is among the 30 largest cities. Both cities make regular appearances on lists of U.S. leading cities. Well over half of the state's residents (about 5.5 million people) live in the Phoenix metropolitan area. The city of Phoenix with 1.3 million residents is the state's largest city. The metro Phoenix area ranks as the 14th largest in the country. In the western states, Phoenix is the 4th largest metro area after Los Angeles, San Francisco, and Seattle. Tucson with a population of 507,000 and Mesa with 427,000 residents are the state's next largest cities. Less than half of Phoenix area residents have lived in the state more than 20 years.

Most of the state's residents live on just 2 percent of the state's land. Actually less than one-fifth of the state is available for private and corporate use. The remainder of the state is under the jurisdiction of state and federal government agencies or Indian nations.

Arizona has been growing by leaps and bounds since the early 1950s. Warm weather, beautiful scenery, and a prospering economy contribute to Arizona's reputation as a growth hot spot. Entire families have migrated to the Grand Canyon State. Parents came to retire, then convinced their children and grandchildren to come. Employees were transferred to Arizona and later brothers, sisters, mothers and fathers, aunts and uncles came to try Arizona.

Arizona's Largest Cities

City	Population	County
Phoenix	1,365,675	Maricopa
Tucson	507,085	Pima
Mesa	427,550	Maricopa
Glendale	227,495	Maricopa
Scottsdale	214,090	Maricopa
Chandler	194,390	Maricopa
Tempe	159,425	Maricopa
Gilbert	133,640	Maricopa
Peoria	122,655	Maricopa
Yuma	81,380	Yuma
Flagstaff	59,160	Coconino
Avondale	47,601	Maricopa
Lake Havasu City	46,400	Mohave
Surprise	45,125	Maricopa
Sun City	45,000	Maricopa
Sierra Vista	40,415	Cochise
Prescott	36,375	Yavapai
Bullhead City	35,410	Mohave
Oro Valley	34,050	Pima
Apache Junction	33,570	Pinal
Casa Grande	27,830	Pinal
Goodyear	26,715	Maricopa
Prescott Valley	26,115	Yavapai
Green Valley	25,410	Pima
Sun City West	25,358	Maricopa
Kingman	22,045	Mohave
Fountain Hills	22,045	Mohave
Nogales	21,110	Santa Cruz

Source: Arizona Department of Economic Security
2002 Population Estimates

With thousands of unpaid recruiters inviting newcomers to the state, you can easily see why the Arizona Department of Economic Security Population Statistics Unit expects Arizona to have 4.8 million residents by the turn of the century. The Bureau of the

Census predicts that Arizona's population will reach 6.4 million by 2025. When the first census was taken in 1869, there were a mere 6,482 inhabitants. By the time Arizona became a state in 1912, the number had grown to 200,000.

While Phoenix and Tucson have blossomed under the Arizona skies, the suburban areas of Phoenix have also grown at incredible rates. All but two of Arizona's ten largest cities are in Maricopa County.

DECIDING FACTORS

People seeking sunshine, warm air and employment opportunities choose the state's southern areas, where 85 percent of the population resides. Cold winters in the nation's Midwest and Northwest are responsible for many decisions to move to southern Arizona. People come with hopes of never, ever needing a snow blower, ice scraper or rock salt again. Earthquakes, floods and poor economic conditions in other parts of the country motivate others to move.

Newcomers seeking a small-town environment in the midst of some of the world's most dramatic natural settings select the four-season northern regions of Arizona where Prescott, Payson, Flagstaff, and Sedona are located. But it's not all basking in the heat, the White Mountains in northeastern Arizona could readily challenge even a Minnesota winter. (While a bit nippy in the winter, the region's lakes and streams offer exceptional summer fishing.)

Newcomers to Phoenix and Tucson come mainly from California, the Midwest and Middle Atlantic states. While new residents in rural Arizona come mainly from the Pacific and Rocky Mountain states.

Arizona's Counties

County	Population
Apache	70,105
Cochise	124,040
Coconino	125,420
Gila	53,015
Graham	34,070
Greenlee	8,605
La Paz	20,365
Maricopa	3,296,250
Mohave	166,465
Navajo	101,615
Pima	890,545
Pinal	192,395
Santa Cruz	39,840
Yavapai	180,260
Yuma	169,760
Arizona	**5,472,750**

Source: Arizona Department of Economic Security
2002 Population Estimates

OPPORTUNITY

To many newcomers, Arizona is the land of opportunity. You'll find a pioneering spirit among the state's residents. Some consider the state one of the few remaining frontiers where the enterprising have a chance to make their fortune. One Arizonan described the state as having a "can do" attitude. A combination of work opportunities and a relaxing lifestyle attract many newcomers and provide incentives for Arizona's youth to remain in the state.

LIFESTYLE

Whether you're in a rural village or an urban center, you'll find the emphasis on relaxation. Since Arizona is one of the nation's vacation playgrounds, people have flocked to the state to kick back

Arizona's Counties

and enjoy themselves. Residents have taken their cue and adopted a philosophy of taking time to stop and enjoy the beauty that surrounds them. With the state's accommodating climate for outdoor activities, Arizonans step out their front doors into one gigantic recreation room.

Visitors are often struck by the practical approach Arizonans take to life and the innovative ways they deal with the warm summer temperatures. Even the finer restaurants take a relaxed approach to dress. You'll seldom be asked to find a tie or put on a jacket.

In the summer, outdoor workers get an early start so they can finish work before the heat of the day. Whether they're off for a siesta or a cool drink in the shade, the day ends early. Most offices have flexible dress codes that put workers' comfort before formality. You'll find most suit coats make their way to the back of the closet between April and September.

Phoenix Art Museum.

Downtown Tucson. (Courtesy of Debs Metzong)

Chapter 2
ARIZONA AT A GLANCE

Stretching 400 miles from top to bottom and 310 miles across, Arizona is the nation's 6th largest state. The state encompasses 113,417 square miles, 492 of which is water. By comparison, all six New England states plus Pennsylvania and Delaware would fit nicely within Arizona's borders.

The state has a low population density. There are vast areas of wide open, uninhabited space. People are concentrated in just a few areas, largely because of the complexity of supplying water to the desert and the large amount of public lands. On the average 45.2 people occupy each square mile of Arizona, although that figure can be a little misleading, since Maricopa County has 334 people sharing each square mile.

CLIMATE

Pleasant weather is one of the prime reasons people move to Arizona. Even in the cold regions of the state, the sun shines brightly day after day. Wherever you are in Arizona, it's only a short drive to a change of scene. Variations in altitude and terrain account for some of the most diverse weather patterns in the nation, but sunshine is the common denominator. On occasion, both the nation's high and low temperature readings are registered in Arizona on the same day.

Number of Days of Inclement Weather for U.S. Cities

Cities	Average Number of Days	
	Rain	Below Freezing
Phoenix	36	11
Boston	114	60
Chicago	125	120
Minneapolis	113	157
New York	119	81
Seattle	152	16

Source: National Weather Service

Average Yearly Precipitation for Arizona Cities

City	Snowfall (Inches)	Rain (Inches)
Phoenix	Trace	7.10
Tucson	0.6	10.73
Flagstaff	84.4	19.80
Yuma	None	2.99
Prescott	23.7	18.10
Sedona	8.8	17.15
Lake Havasu City	None	3.82
Casa Grande	None	8.12

Source: National Weather Service

Summer in southern Arizona is hot and dry, but winters are warm and pleasant. Air conditioning permits residents to live in year-round comfort. Before air conditioning, desert dwellers slept on cots in their backyards or on sleeping porches to escape the heat. They'd dampen the sheets before turning in for the night and hope to fall asleep before the sheets dried. Arizonans began to see some relief in the 1930s when the oscillating fan became available and Phoenix resident Oscar Palmer began the commercial manufacture of evaporative coolers. Home air conditioning was introduced in the 1950s. The air conditioner did more to entice newcomers to Arizona than anything else. Summer temperatures in Tucson are about six degrees cooler than Phoenix.

Since the sun shines four out of every five days, its presence or absence accounts for dramatic temperature differences. In the summer, when daytime temperatures frequently pass 100 degrees, residents rise early or delay outdoor activities until sunset. Joggers, dog walkers, and bicyclists are out at the first sign of light when the summer day is at it's coolest. At twilight, children come out to play, adults head for the stores, and the neighborhoods come alive.

When the eastern portions of the United States are sweltering under summer's damp, sultry conditions day and night, Arizona is often more tolerable even at higher temperatures. There's no denying, some days are just plain hot! (No one will ever try to convince you that June 26, 1990 wasn't warm. The mercury climbed to 122 degrees in Phoenix and the weather records came tumbling down. Even the planes at Sky Harbor International Airport stopped flying.)

Since the temperature drops when the sun goes down, evening temperatures are generally comfortable. You'll have the patio all to yourself on an Arizona summer evening, without screens or insect repellant. Flies and mosquitoes don't seem to care for the heat. At Arizona's higher elevations, summer days are mild with crisp evenings.

Newcomers often ask, "Just how hot is it?" Tolerance for heat varies from individual to individual. There's no easy way to predict how you will adjust to a southern Arizona summer. One indicator, however, may be how you tolerate winter weather. If cold winter weather makes you miserable, you'll probably tolerate the Arizona heat much better than someone who enjoys the cold. Your body does accommodate to its new environment over time. Your first year in the desert many not be a true indicator of how you'll make the transition. After a few years in southern Arizona you may find yourself looking for a sweater when the temperature drops to a cool 80 degrees.

You'll often hear the state's summer weather described as "a dry heat." The low humidity cools your body more efficiently by allowing perspiration to evaporate quickly. You'll feel more comfortable at the higher temperature than at the lower temperature/high humidity level.

The Apparent Temperature chart shows the effect humidity has on how warm the temperature actually seems. During the winter months the effects of low relative humidity are less noticeable, although you may need additional moisturizing lotion for your skin and a conditioner for your hair. Colds seem to go away faster and feel less severe because of the low humidity.

In winter, sunset can mean a rapid drop in temperatures. Temperatures in Phoenix and Tucson occasionally dip below freezing. Northern Arizona, with altitudes above 4,000 feet, has four distinctive seasons. Annual snowfall ranges from just over 8 inches in Sedona to 84 inches in Flagstaff. Summers are cool and pleasant while winters in the high country are cold. Downhill and cross-country skiing entice metropolitan residents to Arizona's high country all winter long. January highs average 42 degrees in Flagstaff and 55 degrees in Sedona. At the higher altitudes air conditioners are not even needed in the summer.

If you have the time, it's a good idea to visit the area of the state that you plan to move to at different seasons. It will give you a much better idea of how you will like the weather conditions.

If southern Arizona is your final destination, a midsummer visit is highly recommended. Summer is an economical time to come. The resorts lower room rates and everyone is glad to see you. You'll even find that many of the guests are local residents on a weekend getaway close to home.

Apparent Temperature

Humidity (%)   **Air Temperature (In Degrees)**

	80	85	90	95	100	105	110	115
0%	73	78	83	87	91	95	99	103
10%	75	80	85	90	95	100	105	111
20%	77	82	87	93	99	105	112	120
30%	78	84	90	96	104	113	123	135
40%	79	86	93	101	110	123	137	151
50%	81	88	96	107	120	135	150	
60%	82	90	100	114	132	149		
70%	85	93	106	124	144			
80%	86	97	113	136				
90%	88	102	122					
100%	91	108						

HEALTH

Many residents first came to Arizona in pursuit of better health. You'll find conflicting opinions, however, about whether the climate will improve your health. Once considered a haven for allergy sufferers, many new residents arrive with sniffles and sneezes, find temporary relief, and then develop a reaction to a new set of local pollens. Unfortunately, some non-indigenous trees and plants have become year-round pollen-bearers. The most notorious of these plants are Bermuda grass, olive trees, and mulberry trees. Tucson even bans the trouble-making plants and imposes penalties if homeowners allow their grass to go to seed. Payson and Prescott promote the healthful aspects of the local pine-filtered air.

City air quality has improved in the past few years. Maricopa and Pima Counties both have auto emissions testing programs, which require owners to keep their vehicles operating cleanly. Maricopa County requires vehicles to use oxygenated-fuels between October and March. Air inversions occur on cold mornings. A cool layer of air traps warm air in the valleys making it difficult for car exhaust and other pollutants to disperse.

If you're considering a move to Arizona for health reasons, you should check with your doctor to see whether a move to a hot-to-cool, dry climate would be beneficial to your condition. Although a few ailments may be aggravated by the climate here, stories of improved health are plentiful. Whether that can be attributed to the low humidity, the heat, the sunshine, or just a change in attitude, no one can be sure.

SNOWBIRDS

For the same reasons people move to Arizona, large numbers of extended vacationers arrive each fall. Natives and residents affectionately refer to the thousands of winter visitors who "flock" to the state when snow begins to fly in the Midwest, Northeast and Canada as "snowbirds."

Close to 30 million visitors come to Arizona each year, contributing billions of dollars to the state's economy. About 200,000 snowbirds "nest" in the Phoenix metropolitan area each February making a significant contribution to the local economy.

Many winter visitors stay in mobile homes and RV parks. About 100,000 mobile home spaces are located in the Phoenix area. Many are in the East Valley, particularly East Mesa and Apache Junction. Yuma, Casa Grande, Tucson and Quartzsite are other popular winter visitor destinations. In addition, many visitors stay in hotels, apartments and with relatives.

The Midwest, upper Northwest, Alaska and Canada are the summer homes of many Arizona snowbirds. Many are from rural areas and small towns. For some the annual pilgrimage starts just after the Christmas holidays and ends shortly before it is time to file their tax returns in April.

GEOGRAPHY

Occasionally, newcomers unacquainted with Arizona arrive expecting to find a barren, Sahara-style desert. They soon discover that there aren't many sand dunes here, although there is an abundance of sand and rock. Arizona's Sonoran desert is filled with life and vegetation. The state has three distinctive topographic regions:

- High plateau area
- Mountainous area
- Desert valley and low mountainous area

Arizona's Geographic Regions

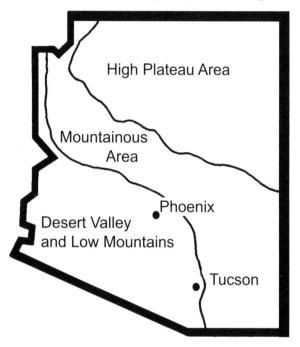

Arizona is roughly divided diagonally from the northwestern corner to southeastern tip. The desert valleys and the low mountains are in the south. Mountains and canyons in the northern high country break long stretches of plateau. The highest point, Humphrey's Peak near Flagstaff, reaches 12,663 feet and the lowest point near Yuma is only 70 feet above sea level.

The Colorado River and its tributaries have cut beautiful canyons into the otherwise flat land of northern Arizona. In addition to the Grand Canyon, other breathtaking canyons include Oak Creek, Canyon de Chelly and Walnut Canyon.

The Salt River Canyon north of Globe on US 60 bears a striking resemblance to the Grand Canyon with its vertical rock walls, multicolored spires, and buttes. The drive winds right down into the canyon dropping more than 2,000 feet in 5 miles of plummeting switchbacks.

The Mogollon (Muggy-OWN) Rim marks the southern boundary of the plateau areas. An awesome geological fault, the Rim is a steep rock wall nearly 2,000 feet high, extending east/west from southwestern New Mexico to central Arizona. Its multicolored rock walls are sprinkled with pine, manzanita, and shrub oak. Southern Arizonans often head for the Rim in midsummer to refresh their spirits in the midst of the world's largest stand of Ponderosa pine.

Nearly a quarter of the state (30,000 square miles) is covered by mountains. The San Francisco Peaks near Flagstaff and the White Mountains in eastern Arizona are the most prominent. Other significant ranges include the Hualapai (WAHL-uh-pie) Mountains south of Kingman, the Bradshaws near Sedona, the Superstitions east of Phoenix, and the Catalinas just outside of Tucson. Many of the mountains are covered with trees, but dry desert mountains,

Superstition Mountains.

with creosote bushes, palo verde trees and cactus are also common. Arizona is one of the few states with six biomes or life zones. The Lower Sonoran Zone has elevations under 4,500 feet, is hot and dry with arid plains, barren mountains and stands of saguaro cactus. Animals retreat to a den or burrow during the heat of the day. In contrast, the Alpine Zone found in the San Francisco Peaks can bring freezing temperatures even in midsummer. Dwarf plants and trees characterize this zone. On Mt. Graham in eastern Arizona, you can visit five life zones in one small area.

WATER

Even in this desert state there are rivers and lakes. Arizona's great water lifeline is the Colorado River. It runs through 688 miles of the state, flowing down from Utah, winding through the Grand Canyon, then turning south to divide Arizona and California. Since 1985 the Central Arizona Project (CAP), has been delivering water from the Colorado River to Phoenix. The 190-mile stretch had been under development since 1968. CAP reached Tucson in 1991 when the remaining 143-mile waterline was completed. CAP is slated to deliver 1.5 million-acre feet into Arizona's interior each year for the cities, farms and Indian reservations. (An acre foot of water is 325,851 gallons.) Water is also available from the Salt River Project, wells, and ground water.

Bridges over dry river beds look strange to new Arizonans, but in a thunderstorm, waterless rivers can quickly become raging torrents. The Salt River runs through Phoenix. Most of the time the water is held behind dams in the canyons or is channeled through the city by the Salt River Project canals. The Salt meets the Verde River east of Phoenix and flows into the Gila River at Gila Bend in western Arizona. Tucson has three major rivers or washes—the Santa Cruz River, Rillito River and Pantano Wash.

Many mountain creeks flow all year. Arizona has 67 natural and man-made lakes. All the state's larger lakes are man-made. They include Roosevelt and San Carlos Lakes, Lake Mead, Lake Havasu and Lake Powell. Lakes Powell and Mead have the distinction of being the two largest artificial lakes in America.

GEOLOGY

Throughout the state rare geological formations provide endless challenges for explorers. A hike from the rim to the river at the Grand Canyon will take you through centuries of geological change.

In Arizona rocks of all sizes, shapes, and derivations are abundant. The most common mineral is copper. Gold, petroleum, pumice, silver, uranium, and zinc also occur naturally, as do gemstones, such as turquoise, fire agate, peridot, amethyst, and opal.

Arizona produces more copper than any other state and is the leading state in the production of gemstones. Both commercial operators and rockhounds find treasure in the state. Turquoise, peridot and petrified wood account for the most valuable commercially harvested Arizona gemstones. Amethyst, chrysocolla, azurite, malachite, fire agate, obsidian and smithsonite also contribute. Although gold and silver are also mined in Arizona sand and gravel are among the state's most valuable commercial resources.

NATIVE AMERICANS

Indian tribes own 19,555,000 acres of reservation land within Arizona's borders. About two-thirds of tribal members live on the reservations. Many others live and work in other parts of the state. Total enrollment for Arizona Indian tribes is 266,000. Tribal enrollment varies from the 224-member San Juan Pauite's to more than

175,000 Navajo tribal members.

Each of the state's 20 reservations is a sovereign nation within the boundaries of the United States, with its own tribal government, laws, culture and customs. Visitors to the reservations are under the jurisdiction of tribal, not Arizona state law. The reservations are administered by the Bureau of Indian Affairs. In recent years, the tribal councils have taken a more active role in governing the reservations, dealing with local, state and federal governments and negotiating with private industry.

In 1924, the Indian Citizenship Act gave citizenship rights to every Native American born within the territorial United States. All Native Americans have full voting rights. Native Americans living on reservations pay all federal and states tax, but do not pay tax on reservation lands and property. Native Americans who do not live on reservations pay the same taxes as other citizens. Indian land is not under state law unless a federal law places it under state law. The Supreme Court has held that even if a tribe is under state law the state gaming regulations do not apply on Indian trust land. In 1988 Congress passed the Indian Gaming Regulatory Act. These laws allow traditional Indian gaming as well as bingo, pull tabs, lotto, punchboards, tip jars and certain card games on tribal lands. However, it requires a tribal/state compact for other forms of gaming such as cards or slot machines. Several Indian tribes operate casinos in Arizona.

Arizona's Native Americans are internationally known for their woven tapestries, basketry, jewelry, pottery, Kachina dolls, sand paintings, and other artwork.

Chapter 3
ARIZONA'S RICH LEGACY

Arizona is a unique blend of the ancient and the ultramodern. Today, aerospace workers engineer components for space stations while other Arizonans live much as their ancestors did hundreds of years ago.

ANCIENT DESERT DWELLERS

Scientists and archaeologists know this region cradled many early life forms. In 1984, 225-million-year-old dinosaur bones were unearthed in northern Arizona's Petrified Forest. The small dog-like dinosaur, nicknamed "Gertie" by the scientists who found her, roamed the state during the Triassic Age, 100 million years before there were flowers and trees on earth. Turtle fossils were found near the northern Arizona community of Kayenta which are believed to be the oldest of their kind in North America, about 185 million years old.

When compared to other life forms, people are relative newcomers to the state. Primitive man lived in Arizona 50,000 years ago. Some early Arizona residents migrated from Asia to Alaska and then moved southward. Others may have moved up from South America.

NATIVE AMERICANS

Centuries before the first European explorers edged their ships toward the shores of the New World, ancestors of many of today's tribal groups already resided in Arizona. Three groups settled the area that became Arizona. The Anasazi lived in the northern plains, the Hohokam in the arid central region of the Salt and Gila River valleys and the Mogollon lived among the streams and forests of eastern Arizona.

Between the time of Christ and 1300 A.D. the Anasazi occupied the Four Corners region where Arizona, New Mexico, Utah and Colorado meet. They were the ancestors of the Hopi and Pueblo Indians. The Hopi village of Old Oraibi in northern Arizona was built in 1100 A.D. and has been continuously inhabited since that time. 500 years later the Pilgrims landed at Plymouth Rock. The Anasazi left behind extensive artifacts including pottery, turquoise, jewelry, woven baskets, cotton clothing, stone tools, and mummies.

By 200 A.D., an agricultural tribe, known as the Hohokam, migrated to Arizona. During their thousand-year stay, the Hohokam built a complex system of irrigation canals. The Hohokam suddenly disappeared about the time Columbus was setting sail for the New World. The Tohono O'Odham and Pima who now live in southern Arizona are believed to be descendants of the Hohokams. The word Arizona is thought to have come from ali shonak which means "small place of the spring" in the Tohono O'Odham language.

EXPLORERS, MISSIONARIES AND
FRONTIERSMEN

In the sixteenth century, Spanish explorers, including Coronado, came north from Mexico in search of the gold-plated Seven Cities of

Cibola. Until the 17th century, the region was sparsely populated with Native American settlements.

Shortly before European settlers came, the Athapascan-speaking people (the Apache and Navajo) arrived. Late in the seventeenth century Father Eusibio Kino, a Jesuit priest, established missions in Arizona. The most famous, the Mission San Xavier del Bac "White Dove of the Desert," near Tucson is still in use today.

Spanish troops established the first European settlement at Tubac in 1752. A few years later in 1776, a Spanish fort and missionary outpost were set up at Tucson. In the following 80 years, the area that was to become Arizona passed from Spain to Mexico to the United States. Land north of the Gila River was ceded to the United States with the Treaty of Guadalupe Hidalgo in 1848. In 1853 the Gadsden Purchase obtained additional land from Mexico to construct a railroad.

Mission San Xavier del Bac.

Congress passed a bill creating the Arizona Territory on December 17, 1863. President Abraham Lincoln signed the bill in February of the next year. At about the same time, Anglo settlers rediscovered the area once inhabited by the Hohokam and established the city of Phoenix. Tucson was already a vital southern supply depot and was the territorial capital.

Early settlers fought bitterly with raiding Indians bands. Cochise, Geronimo, and Mangas Colorados were among the well-known Apache chiefs. Under Geronimo's leadership, the Apaches finally surrendered on September 4, 1886, 2 years after the Navajo surrendered to Kit Carson. This era is a controversial one in the state's history and still a painful one for many of the state's residents.

Descendants of the early Spanish, Mexican, and Native American settlers still live in Arizona. Their cultural contributions can be seen in the architecture, food, clothing, decorating, art, language, and lifestyle of the Southwest.

Shortly before the Civil War, miners flooded Arizona's streams and wooded mountains in search of gold and silver. Prescott, Wickenburg, the Superstition Mountains, Cave Creek, and even the Grand Canyon were swarming with fortune seekers. While only a few struck it rich, many stayed and became farmers, ranchers, and businessmen.

In the late 1860s, farmers in the Salt River Valley began irrigating their fields and in the next 10 years ranching became big business. Copper mines flourished in the 1870s and 1880s.

Arizona lobbied Washington for statehood diligently for 23 years between 1889 and 1912. While Democrats in both houses of Congress generally favored statehood for Arizona, Republicans were reluctant to admit a state filled with wild frontiersmen. Arizonans favored free coinage of silver and the vote for women. They wanted initiative, referendums and recall provisions in their constitution. Conservative members of Congress were uncomfortable with these Arizona views. Finally, on February 14, 1912, Arizona became the 48th state, the last continental state to join the Union. Arizona is known both as the Valentine State and as the Baby State. Since 1912, government has evolved considerably. (Or so we'd like to think!) Arizona has never lacked for colorful political figures. In the recent past the state's governors have been the subject of recall, impeachment and even indictment. The Arizona state flag is an eyecatcher. The lower half of the flag is blue, and the upper half is divided into thirteen equal segments, alternating red and yellow. The center of the flag is a copper-colored star. The red and blue represent the United States. Blue and yellow are the Arizona colors. Red and yellow were the colors of the Spanish Conquistadors who explored Arizona in 1540. The copper star represents Arizona as the nation's largest copper producer.

Saguaro Cactus Blossom, Arizona State Flower.
(Courtesy of Debs Metzong)

Officially Arizona

State Flower	Saguaro Cactus Blossom
State Tree	Palo Verde
State Songs	*Arizona March Song* and *Arizona*
State Gem	Turquoise
State Bird	Cactus Wren
State Fossil	Petrified Wood
State Mammal	Ringtail
State Reptile	Arizona Ridge-nosed Rattlesnake
State Fish	Apache Trout
State Amphibian	Arizona Treefrog
State Neckwear	Bola Tie
State Capitol	Phoenix
State Motto	Ditat Deus (God Enriches)
State Nickname	Grand Canyon State

Chapter 4

BRINGING HOME THE BACON

Thousands of job seekers descend on Arizona each year lured by the promise of potential employment. Nearly half of Arizona's newcomers cite employment opportunities as the deciding factor in their move to the state.

The Sun Belt leads the nation as the region expected to have the greatest job growth in the coming years. Job growth and total personal income growth has outpaced national averages. Arizona job growth over the past several years has been one of the best in the country. A well-trained labor force, good housing, good transportation, a friendly regulatory climate, a stable political climate, and politicians who are willing to work out incentive policies reduce the cost of doing business in Arizona. In recent years the state has expanded worker-training, and incentives for environmental, defense-related, high tech and mining companies.

Despite good growth numbers, don't expect salaries to be as high as in the coastal areas. Arizona has a long history of below average pay that it is still trying to overcome. If you are not a high tech worker, you may still find yourself underpaid. Average annual pay is still below the national average. Workers were often told they were being paid in sunshine. That is beginning to change. Average personal income has been growing at about 7-8 percent in recent years. It still falls in the mid-range of Western states. Several factors contribute to the lower than national income levels including:

- Arizona's Right To Work laws.
- Ease of attracting new employees.
- Fewer high paying manufacturing jobs, and
- Large numbers of retirees, not earning salaries.

Offsetting personal income levels are lower cost of living expenses, which are generally less than in other Western states. Recent figures showed Phoenix almost 5 percent below the national average and Tucson 3 percent below the national average. Those compare with Los Angeles at 37 percent above and San Diego at 38 percent above and even Denver at 5 percent above national averages.

Your best break will probably come on your housing expenses. The National Association of Realtors compiles figures on the median housing prices in U.S. metropolitan areas. Average prices at the end of 2002 were $145,800 in Phoenix and $149,400 in Tucson. For the same time period Chicago was $223,300, Los Angeles $304,600 and Seattle $258,300. The national average was $161,600. You'll also find utility expenses are below national averages. The Phoenix metro area has also benefited from intense competition for the consumer's grocery dollar.

If current patterns continue, more than 80 percent of the new jobs will be created in the Phoenix or Tucson metropolitan areas. Currently, Maricopa and Pima Counties account for more than 80 percent of all economic activity in the state although many strategies have been developed to promote development in other Arizona communities. The economies of some rural areas such as

Yuma, Lake Havasu City, Kingman, Bullhead City and Prescott Valley are also growing rapidly. If big city life isn't your cup of tea, you'll find lots of incentives for setting up shop in the rural communities and on Arizona Indian reservations. Both population growth and the business climate give Arizona a bright outlook for jobs from now until well into the twenty-first century.

BUSINESS CLIMATE

Arizona's unemployment rate has traditionally been slightly lower than the national average. Unemployment rates for the cities of Phoenix and Tucson are even lower, since higher unemployment rates in rural Arizona bring up the state's overall rate.

Low unemployment is due in part to the broad base of economic activity that insulates Arizona from bad times in any particular industry. Personal income, retail sales, bank deposits, and value-added manufacturing output have grown at an even faster rate than the population in the past decade. Among the largest one hundred cities in the U.S., Phoenix and Tucson are in the lowest 5 percent when it comes to tax burden. The state's corporate tax rate was lowered from 9 to 8 percent in 1998. And the personal income tax has slid by more than 30 percent in the past few years.

EMPLOYMENT STRUCTURE

Arizona's economy largely depends on manufacturing, tourism, and services. Technology related industries have been a major force in recent years. More than 50 percent of the state's manufacturing jobs are technology-related compared to 20 percent nationally. The same industry accounts for about 75 percent of the state's exports. Salaries in the high tech industry are a driving force in raising the

Arizona's Employment Sectors

Mining	>1%
Information (Publishing, Telecommunications)	2%
Transportation	3%
Agriculture, Forestry, Fisheries	3%
Finance, Insurance, Real Estate	7%
Construction	8%
Manufacturing	8%
Tourism	10%
Trade	16%
Government	18%
Service	24%

Source: Arizona Department of Economic Security,
    Research Division

state's personal income levels. Arizona has numerous electronics industry employers in all segments of the industry including computer, semiconductor, software, consumer electronics, telecommunications equipment, medical electronics, and defense-electronics.

The service sector is the largest, as well as the state's fastest-growing industry. Nearly a quarter of all Arizona jobs and personal income derive from industries providing services.

Tourism remains another mainstay in the Arizona economy. World-class destination resorts are located in the Phoenix, Tucson, and Sedona areas.

Mining and agriculture, while significant, account for a very small percentage of economic activity. In Arizona a few hundred large farms account for about 80 percent of agricultural production. The state's most important commodities are cotton, milk, and beef. Other significant crops included oranges, lemons, lettuce, wheat, and alfalfa. Together agriculture and mining contribute less than 2 percent of Arizonans' personal income. Arizona copper mines produce 65 percent of the copper mined in the United States.

EXPERT ADVICE

Not everyone who comes to Arizona, however, finds the job he or she wants immediately. (For every three people who move to Arizona, two move away.) A preliminary visit to the state is highly advisable. It's important to come prepared. Nearly a third of newcomers have a job lined up before arriving. Fewer than 10 percent of newcomers arrive without a reasonable assurance of a job. If you plan to move to Arizona before you have a job, you should be financially prepared to weather a few months (3-6 months) of unemployment. It is dififcult for some non-resident job seekers, while others find jobs plentiful. Usually, the easiest jobs to find pay less and require fewer skills.

Successful job seekers have given themselves an advantage in the job market. They have:
- Secured the proper licensing.
- Identified the type of job they want.
- Identified and researched potential employers.
- Visited the business section of the public library to re-search employers, industries, products and services in the area.
- Used the Internet to research employers, industries, products and services in the area.
- Read industry trade publications.
- Joined local professional associations.
- Sought assistance from local unions.
- Contacted the local chamber of commerce.

- Checked to see what is available at the One-Stop Career Centers.
- Joined community organizations.
- Studied the newspaper classified sections.
- Examined related listings in the yellow pages.

To obtain background information on a particular company, write to the company's public relations department and ask for company brochures and stockholders reports. This information may also be available at the public library or on the Internet.

Many professional and trade associations maintain job banks for their members. Some associations will allow non-members access to the job listings for a fee. Contact any national associations you now belong to for information regarding Arizona affiliates.

Some local chamber of commerce offices maintain lists of

Arizona Occupations Expected to Have the Most Openings

Cashiers
Retail Salespersons
Office Clerks
Secretaries, not legal or Medical
Waiters/Waitresses
Marketing and Sales Worker Supervisors
Janitors and Cleaners
Registered Nurses
Office and Administrative Support
Supervisors and Managers
Bookkeeping, Accounting and Auditing Clerks

Source: Arizona Department of Economic Security
         (1998 - 2008 projections)

employers. You will discover that many job openings are never advertised in the newspapers. If you expect to find out about these openings you'll need an inside track. Many successful job seekers credit networking with finding their positions. That is, they attend business and social functions that enable them to meet people with whom they can exchange information and advice.

Two of the best sources for obtaining an overview of what is happening in Arizona's business and economic worlds are websites maintained by the department of commerce and the department of economic security's research administration. Search for the official state of Arizona website and you'll be able to find both of these sites readily.

The Arizona Department of Economic Security operates

Arizona Hourly Average Wages

Occupation	Hourly Rate
Accountant	$21.59
Artists	17.47
Auto Mechanic	14.85
Carpenter	15.34
Civil Engineer	26.78
Computer Programmer	25.49
Cook, Restaurant	9.01
Dietitians	18.27
Electricians	16.42
LP Nurse	14.67
Machinist	15.01
Receptionist	9.27
Registered Nurse	22.63
Retail Sales	10.63
Stock Clerk	9.45
Systems Analyst	31.25
Truck Drivers (Heavy)	16.45
Welder	12.78
Source: Arizona Dept. of Economic Security, Research Division	

One-Stop Career Centers throughout the state. The State of Arizona has many resources for job seekers and those who seek employees. Each county is now linked to the One-Stop Career Center. Department of Labor programs and services are integrated in one location. These include Job Service, Veteran's Employment and Training, Job Training Partnership Act for disadvantaged adults and youth and for those who have lost jobs due to layoffs or plant closures. In addition, the centers administer unemployment insurance benefits and employment and training for anyone fifty-five or older.

For job seekers there is help with selecting a career, obtaining job training information, finding a job, applying for unemployment benefits and finding child care.

For employers there is help with finding employees, locating information about tax credits and wage reimbursements, helping employees find child care, accommodating disabled workers, tax credits for certain groups of workers, and labor market information such as wage surveys and hiring trends.

For a list One-Stop Career Center locations, see Appendix A.

REGISTRATION, CERTIFICATION AND LICENSING

Certain occupations require special licenses to transact business. Various agencies, boards, and offices are responsible for administering these licenses. For details see Appendix C.

RIGHT TO WORK

In Arizona, a Right-to-Work statute prohibits compulsory union membership. The percentage of union workers in Arizona is only about half of what it is nationally. You'll hear mixed reviews about the Right to Work law. On one hand it has contributed to Arizona's economic growth, and on the other hand it has also limited workers' recourse. Overall, most Arizonans favor the law, believing that without it many companies would have chosen to locate elsewhere. One count showed that fewer than 5 percent of Arizona employees in the manufacturing sector belonged to unions.

EMPLOYEE RIGHTS

It pays to keep former Arizona employers aware of your current address. In Arizona, it is illegal for an employer to "blacklist" someone and prevent that person from working. Employers may exchange information about an employee's education, training, experience, qualifications, and job performance. An employer, however, must send a copy of any written communication to the former employee's last known address. Change of address notices sent by certified mail will assure that you are notified when your past and future employers exchange information.

ESTABLISHING A BUSINESS

Establishing a business in the state of Arizona is a relatively simple process. The most common legal structures for Arizona businesses are the sole proprietorship, partnership, limited partnership, and corporation.

Sole proprietorships, which do business under a name other than the owner's, need to register the business name with the Secretary of State's office.

General partnerships operating under a fictitious name should do likewise. Some partnerships are exempt. To obtain more information consult the Arizona Revised Statutes.

Limited partnerships, domestic or foreign, should register with the Arizona Secretary of State's Office. Trademarks are also registered with the Secretary of State.

For more information contact:

> Secretary of State
> 1700 W. Washington St.
> Phoenix, AZ 85007
> (602) 542-4285

Corporations must file Articles of Incorporation with the Arizona Corporation Commission.

The following steps are required:

- Make sure that the name you are using has been checked with the Commission and is available for use by your corporation.
- Deliver the original and one or more copies of the Articles of Incorporation to the Commission.
- Show a street address for the statutory agent.
- File a certificate of disclosure.
- Pay the required fees.
- Advise the Commission, in writing, of the fiscal year to be used by the corporation.
- Publish the Articles of Incorporation within 60 days after filing with the Commission.

If the business is a foreign corporation (an entity under the laws of another state or foreign country) it must be registered with the

Arizona Corporation Commission.
For more information contact:
The Arizona Corporation Commission
1300 W. Washington St.
Phoenix, AZ 85007
(602) 542-3026

402 W. Congress St.
Tucson, AZ 85701
(520) 542-3026

The Arizona Commerce Department's Business Assistance Center operates a center, which provides information to anyone relocating or starting a new business. There are special programs for minorities, women, and small businesses. For more information contact:
Arizona Department of Commerce
3800 N. Central Ave. Ste. 1650
Phoenix, AZ 85012
1-800-542-5684

The Arizona Department of Revenue can provide specific details about business taxes and licenses.
For more information contact:
Arizona Department of Revenue
1600 W. Monroe St.
Phoenix, AZ 85007
(602) 542-1991

The Arizona Department of Commerce oversees federal financing for small businesses in Arizona.
For more information contact:

Arizona Department of Commerce
3800 N. Central Ave. Ste. 1650
Phoenix, AZ 85012
(602) 280-1300

The Arizona Department of Commerce has several publications that may be useful publications for anyone considering locating a business in the state including profiles of communities and counties throughout the state. Contact the department for more information.

Chapter 5
A ROOF OVER YOUR HEAD

Arizona, and particularly southern Arizona, has a distinctive architectural and landscaping style. Arizona homes often feature tile roofs, tan stucco buildings, swimming pools, privacy walls, arches, and courtyards.

Stucco, brick, slump block, and cement block are the most commonly used building materials. In the early years, homes were built of adobe with walls two-feet-thick to provide natural insulation from the heat. Today, block, frame and stucco have replaced adobe.

Arizonans take pride in their homes, devoting many hours to upkeep. Because of the year-round access to the outdoors and the emphasis on leisure you'll find gorgeous backyards that truly extend the family's living space to the great outdoors.

Homeowners install automatic sprinkling systems, plant special winter and summer grasses and cultivate a succession of plants and flowers for each season. Interest in outside appearances is responsible for a Phoenix city ordinance that requires homeowners to maintain the appearance of their property.

The temptation when you first arrive in Arizona is to try to replicate the look of the environment you just left behind. While you can grow many plants that are inhabitants of greener parts of the country, try to resist the urge. They are often water guzzlers and because of the warm temperatures may grow much faster and can require more maintenance than you expected as well as create problems they don't have in four-season climates, such as continuous seed production. Because freezing temperatures don't occur every year in all parts of Arizona, some bugs stay around all year to nibble on that precious specimen and that means more trouble. Other plants can't take the heat and will wither and die once summer arrives. While it may take a bit of adjustment at first, there are certainly big dividends for choosing native plants and rock gardens. There's less need to mow, fertilize, or weed. By choosing indigenous plants you won't be introducing plants that are unable to adjust to the climate or need profuse watering.

Many cities have Water Conservation Offices that promote xeriscape landscaping. The term refers to the creative use of plants and landscaping materials for water and energy efficiency. Xeriscape yards typically make use of mulches, low water use plants, and efficient irrigation. They may even feature turf areas, but often as an accent rather than the primary feature.

Check with your city's Water Conservation office to see if there are xeriscape classes in your area. Once you learn the names and can recognize some of the local plants you'll be much more informed on your next trip to the garden center. Keep in mind that the garden centers stock what customers buy. Just because it is in stock, doesn't mean its right for your yard. An ice plant may have been perfect on a California hillside, but it may not be nearly as happy in your Arizona yard.

Citrus flourish in the Arizona desert, but do require lots of water. Orange, grapefruit, and lemon trees are often used as ornamental trees. Many fruits and vegetables do well in Arizona, but newcomers to southern Arizona soon discover that the end of the growing season back home may be just about the right time to begin planting tomatoes and petunias in Arizona. High soil alkalinity and low rainfall complicate matters. Gardens do well here, but it takes a bit of adjusting. The county cooperative extension office may be the best source of information.

There are very few basements in Arizona, and many older homes have carports rather than enclosed garages. Many homes use low, one-story designs. Older homes are generally ranch-style, while newer homes are Spanish-Mediterranean or pueblo-style. Tile roofs are common in more expensive homes, asphalt shingles on less expensive homes. Since heating and cooling ductwork frequently run through the ceiling rather than a basement, air-conditioning or "refrigeration" units and evaporative coolers are sometimes located on rooftops. More expensive homes almost always locate the cooling units on the ground.

Evaporative cooling units, or "swamp coolers," are an Arizona invention which cools by pulling air across water-soaked pads and circulating it through the house. Such coolers are less costly to operate than air conditioners and cool quite efficiently when the temperature is below 100 degrees, and the humidity is low. Evaporative coolers operate best when the dew point is below 55 degrees. Homes are often equipped with both cooling systems, since evaporative coolers are not as efficient during the summer monsoon season.

More than 80 percent of the heating and cooling systems of new homes are powered by an electric heat pump and usually do not include the evaporative system. Heat pumps are energy efficient, operating best when the temperature is higher than 32 degrees. Heat pumps require only one mechanical system. In the winter, the refrigerant circulating inside the heat pump picks up heat from outside air and pumps it into the home. In the summer, heat from inside the home is absorbed and pumped outside. Tests show that heat pumps use about one-fourth the energy of a gas furnace.

Arizona homes generally feature lots of windows and large

covered patios to take maximum advantage of the views. Many residents prefer wood or metal blinds to fabric window coverings since blinds are easier to keep dust-free and allow rooms to be bright, yet shaded. Tile, stone, brick, or flagstone is often used as interior floor covering.

While Arizonans are taming the sun with one hand, they are putting it to work with the other by installing solar heaters that warm both household water and swimming pools. It's an excellent way to get free energy and save on electrical bills. In southern Arizona, you'll want to keep in mind that you'll have higher utility bills in the summer, rather than winter, due to the higher cost of summer cooling and lower cost of winter heating.

Patios and swimming pools also help manage the summer heat. About one in seven homes have a backyard swimming pool. Many apartments include a community pool as an amenity. You'll find an endless variety of styles including play pools, lap pools, and diving pools. Extreme caution is recommended if you have young children. Child drowning and near drowning are preventable. The sparkling water of a backyard pool is utterly irresistible to children. Never leave a child alone with access to a pool, even for a few seconds. See Chapter 9 for details on how to improve safety around your pool. Pool tragedies create multiple problems. Not only is there a loss of life or the severe consequences of a critically injured child, but many families also disintegrate because they are unable to cope with the added emotional and financial stress. Grief, guilt, and blame can become overwhelming.

Many cities and counties have adopted city ordinances that require pools to be enclosed by fencing. Be sure the home you are buying meets these specifications.

Maricopa County Median Sales Price

Ahwatukee/Foothills	$211,666
Apache Junction	129,900
Anthem	232,616
Carefree/Cave Creek	426,868
Chandler	171,000
Fountain Hills	265,000
Gilbert	167,000
Glendale	142,000
Mesa	144,523
Paradise Valley	846,481
Phoenix	162,000
Scottsdale	294,000
Sun City West	137,900
Surprise	133,072
Tempe	169,000

Source: Arizona Center for Real Estate (2002 figures)

HOME OWNERSHIP

Housing choices in Arizona abound and competition for home sales and rentals is keen, which is good news for the newcomer. You'll find a wide variety of housing from multi-million dollar estates to efficiency apartments. There are also townhomes, condominiums, patio homes, traditional homes, planned communities, mobile home parks, and established neighborhoods. There are both brand-new homes and many previously owned homes on the market. As a general rule new homes are slightly higher in cost than resale properties.

Multiple Listing Services allow all agents belonging to the service to sell any home listed. New property is often purchased directly from the builder/developer, but it doesn't cost any more to have a Realtor represent you in the purchase and can prevent you from making an unwise selection, particularly if you are unfamiliar with the local market. What may look like a dirt path leading to that new subdivision, could become a busy street in a few years and hold your property value down if you've chosen a lot that backs up to it. If you want Realtor representation on a new home purchase, be sure to take the Realtor with you the first time you visit the new housing development.

Most home purchase problems can be traced to rushing into the decision, looking at too many homes at one time, or not adequately checking what the home and neighborhood have to offer. If you plan to buy a previously owned home and are not willing to risk unexpected repair bills or other surprises, you can obtain a third-party evaluation from a professional inspection firm. Warranty insurance may also be available. Ask to see the property disclosure statement.

Many newer homes are located in areas with homeowner associations. These groups work to maintain property values through self-policing efforts. Property owners who fail to maintain their property receive notices asking that the problem be corrected. If the homeowner fails to comply the homeowner's association can take the matter to court. Monthly fees paid by all the homeowners whose property is included in the area fund the homeowner's associations. The fees vary by what services are being offered. Some amenities which may be included are: common areas used for biking and walking trails, upgraded landscape along streets, community pools, tennis courts, and in some cases security features. For some homeowners this is a great way to have access to additional amenities without the responsibility of maintaining and monitoring and a way to make sure the neighborhood doesn't go downhill. If you like to park your old vehicles in the front yard for months at a time, let your grass get as tall as an elephant's eye, or even let your garbage can sit out at the curb for a few extra days, you may find the homeowner's association breathing down your neck. Be sure to read the rules and regulations and find out what the fees are before purchasing property.

Because there are so many choices, the best advice is to carefully consider:

- location
- housing type and style
- cost

Ethics complaints and arbitration against a Realtor may be filed with local Boards of Realtors. Arizona has a fund designed to compensate victims of unlawful practices by licensed real estate agents or brokers. Real estate license fees finance the Arizona Real Estate Recovery Fund. The fund authorizes as much as $15,000 for each victim, with a maximum of $30,000 to compensate for the wrongdoing of a particular agent or broker.

To have a claim paid from the fund, you first must sue the agent or broker and obtain a court judgment. You must give proper notice at the time of filing the lawsuit to the Arizona Real Estate Commissioner.

If you win the suit, you are required to make reasonable efforts to collect the judgment directly from the wrongdoer. If you are unable to collect, you may then submit your claim to the Arizona Department of Real Estate, the agency that administers the fund. The Arizona Department of Real Estate is located at:

2910 N. 44th St.

Phoenix, AZ 85018

(602) 468-1414

400 W. Congress St. Ste. 523
Tucson, AZ 85701
(520) 628-6940

Some people prefer to build custom homes. If this avenue appeals to you, check on prospective contractors by contacting:
Registrar of Contractors
800 W. Washington St.
Phoenix, AZ 85007
(602) 542-1525

400 W. Congress
Tucson, AZ 85701
(520) 628-6345

Both residential and commercial contractors must be licensed.

AGE-RESTRICTED ZONING

Arizona allows municipalities to make public ordinances establishing age-specific community zoning districts. In some cases whole communities are affected, and in others just certain developments.

These laws require that the head of the household or spouse be a specific age or older. Age-specific community zoning districts cannot be created over existing property without permission of all property owners in the district unless the property has been developed, advertised, and sold or rented under those restrictions.

Other restrictions may be applied by county and city ordinances as well as deed restrictions. For example, Maricopa County's Senior Citizen Zoning Ordinance makes it illegal for anyone eighteen years of age or younger to live in "senior zones." The Board of Adjustment makes exemptions for hardship conditions only.

Before selecting an age-restrictive community, be sure you understand exactly what the conditions are, how exemptions are made, and what penalties for non-compliance are imposed. Also keep in mind when it is time to resell a home in an age-restricted community you will have a smaller pool of buyers who are eligible to purchase your home and your heirs may be ineligible to live in the home if they don't meet the age restrictions. Many retirement communities are located throughout the state. For more detailed information refer to the book *Retiring in Arizona.*

RENTING

Late spring, summer, and early fall are the best times to apartment hunt. In winter, the large number of seasonal visitors reduces the selection and the prices are higher. You'll find giveaway publications on stands at grocery stores, convenience stores, and some chambers of commerce or visitor's bureaus that list apartment complexes with vacancies and others listing homes for sale. These publications can be very useful in targeting areas and price ranges. Smaller units and homes may be found through the newspaper, drive-by signs, Realtor leasing services or apartment location services. Generally the landlord usually pays the fee for these services. Be sure to inquire about who is paying the fee when you first make contact.

Before you sign any rental agreement, be sure you understand:

- The amount of rent and when it is due.
- The amount of deposit and how much of it is refundable.
- Where you can park.
- Whether the utilities are included in the rent or must be paid for separately.
- The procedure for terminating the lease.
- The rules regarding pets and pet deposits.

- The rules about using common facilities such as pool, laundry, etc.
- Who takes care of pest control.

Wise renters get acquainted with the Arizona Residential Landlord and Tenant Act. To obtain a copy contact:

Secretary of State
1700 W. Washington St.
Phoenix, AZ 85007
(602) 542-4285

The law spells out landlord and tenant obligations. Some of the points covered by the law are discussed here. Before taking any action, read the law yourself or consult a lawyer for advice. The law covers a variety of issues.

In Arizona, the landlord must provide the name of the owner or person authorized to act on the owner's behalf and to whom notices and demands are to be sent. If there is a written rental agreement, both the tenant and the landlord must have copies signed by the other party. Any written rental agreement must have all blank spaces completed.

"Notice" of problems or plans to vacate must be given to the landlord in one of several ways: hand-delivered, mailed by registered or certified mail to the place of business of the landlord through which the rental agreement was made or at any place held as the place where communication is to be sent, or delivered to the designated agent. To terminate a month-to-month rental arrangement, the landlord or tenant must give at least 30 days' notice prior to the periodic rental date. In other words, if you pay your rent on the first of the month and you plan to move October 1, you must notify the landlord before September 1.

An Arizona landlord cannot ask for security and prepaid rent in excess of one and a half month's rent. If cleaning and redecorating deposits are not refundable, it must be so stated in writing. When the tenant moves out, property or money held as security can be applied to accumulated rent and damages. The landlord has 14 days after the tenant moves out to return deposits or provide damage statements.

While the tenant is obligated to provide access to the unit, the landlord is required to give 2 days' notice of intent to enter. The landlord is permitted to enter without consent in case of an emergency. The law provides for remedies if the problems are not taken care of promptly, and enables the tenant to correct other conditions.

MOBILE HOMES

About 10 percent of the state's residents live in mobile homes. Arizona's warm, dry climate makes this an especially popular choice among retirees. Per square foot, mobile homes are generally about a third the cost of conventional housing. Many planned mobile home communities offer sophisticated amenities such as golf courses, saunas, and tennis courts.

The Arizona Office of Manufactured Housing oversees state laws regarding manufactured housing.

For more information contact:

Office of Manufactured Housing
State Department of Building and Fire Safety
99 E. Virginia Ave.
Phoenix, AZ 85004

The Mobile Home Landlord-Tenant Act spells out the rights and responsibilities of landlords and tenants in mobile home parks.

For the latest information, you may obtain a copy of the law by contacting:

> Secretary of State
> 1700 W. Washington St.
> Phoenix, AZ 85007
> (602) 542-4285

Chapter 6
SELECTING A SCHOOL

Like other educational systems across the country Arizona has been working diligently to improve education over the last several years. As with most changes some ideas are better than others, and growth often comes with some pain. New teacher certification rules, new ways of financing education and new ways of assessing student progress have been at the center of the changes. For the most part Arizona has a very sound educational system. Teacher training programs at the state's universities are excellent, with students getting a great deal of in-classroom experience through internships and student teaching. Many Arizona schools are relatively new, and have the advantages of clean, bright surroundings. Inequities in funding are being dealt with to improve the schools in other less affluent areas.

In the past few years there has been a growing movement among community business leaders to work closely with the state's educators to develop ways in which education can be improved. Many schools have been adopted by local businesses and provide assistance in a variety of ways.

Each of Arizona's elementary and high school districts are administered by a school board that is under the general supervision of the Superintendent of Public Instruction. In Arizona, school districts often cross city boundaries, (although many bear the names of communities within the district).

There are three types of school districts: elementary, secondary and unified districts. Property may be in both an elementary and a secondary district. A unified district combines elementary and secondary schools under one administration.

In addition to public schools, students may attend charter schools, private schools, or receive home-based instruction. State law allows parents to send their children to any public school, inside or outside of the child's home districts.

ENROLLMENT REQUIREMENTS

Anyone with custody of a child between the ages of six and sixteen must send the child to school. The child may be enrolled in private school or receive home-based instruction.

AGE REQUIREMENTS

Schools admit children between the ages of six and twenty-one who reside in the school district. A child is considered six years of age if his birthday occurs before September 1 of the current school year. Children five years of age before September 1 are eligible to attend kindergarten. Children with birthdays between September 1 and December 1 may enroll at an earlier age if the parent, child, teacher and principal agree it is in the child's best interest.

IMMUNIZATION REQUIREMENTS

State law requires school children to be immunized for measles, mumps, rubella, diphtheria, tetanus, polio, and Hepatitis B (2 doses). The law requires parents or guardians to present a documented immunization record that includes dates of all required immunizations.

In order to be admitted to school, the child must have at least one current dose of each vaccine and receive the next dose when due. If the required immunizations have not been received, the child is referred to a physician or the county health department. Medical, religious or personal reasons may be given. Medical reasons may require signatures by both the parent and the physician. If there is an outbreak of an illness, however, for which the child is not adequately protected, the child will automatically be excluded from school for the duration of the outbreak. State law also requires child care centers to have immunization records for each attending child.

HOME-BASED INSTRUCTION

Enrollment requirements may be met if your child is instructed at home. For more information about who can be a home-based teacher and requirements for students to take nationally standardized achievement tests contact the County Superintendent of Schools in the county where you reside. If a child attends home school or private school the parent must complete and submit an Affidavit of Intent for each child between the ages of six and sixteen with the county Superintendent of Schools. A child who enrolls in a home school program and later enrolls in the public schools may be tested to determine the appropriate grade and class level. Contact your local public school for their policy regarding enrollment of previously home-schooled students.

CHARTER SCHOOLS

Charter schools are another option for parents. Charter schools support flexibility, and innovation in area of operations and organizational structure. The manner in which they govern, schedule, implement curriculum, and their teaching methods may be quite different from the local public school. In order to receive state funding charter schools must meet certain requirements including financial soundness. Charter schools cannot limit admissions except regarding grades, age groups, and capacity. Teachers in the charter schools are eligible to participate in the state teacher's retirement system.

Charter schools are a relatively recent innovation and their track record is still being established. It is very difficult to generalize about the quality of the programs. For some students they may be an ideal choice, for others it may be less than ideal. The schools are often smaller than public schools with presumably more individual attention. And because they are smaller there are also fewer choices in curriculum and activities. Charter schools often have a particular focus such as the arts or specific teaching styles. If your child's needs match the particular school's focus it may be a perfect match.

PRIVATE SCHOOLS

The Arizona Department of Education publishes an Educational Directory listing all schools in the state. If you are searching for a private school, it may be of help in locating names, addresses, and phone numbers. The Catholic Diocese of Phoenix also has an Office of Education. For more information phone (602) 257-0030. The Arizona Private School Association will provide school names, locations, phone numbers, and lists of available courses for post–secondary schools. For more information contact:

Arizona Private School Association
202 E. McDowell Rd. Ste. 273
Phoenix, AZ 85004
(602) 254-5199

STATEWIDE TESTING

One thing that we can count on changing each time this book is revised is how students are being tested. Without sounding too skeptical, let's summarize the current approach briefly. Primarily, testing is a fundamental and valuable way of assesing the average knowledge and skill level of students. The state's educators, administrators, and legislators seem to think that students should be tested frequently and the results published. For example, Arizona requires students to pass an examination before high school graduation. With this idea in mind, it is also important to remember that the tests should by no means be considered the only comprehensive evaluation of everything that students know or should know. Accordingly, a negative evaluation of any particular school, classroom or even student's achievement on these tests should be made very cautiously. Many teachers feel intense pressure to improve the school's test scores. Any test is simply a snapshot of what was happening on one particular day in one particular classroom with each individual student, but continous testing over a period of time can be positive indicators of what needs improvement for any school district.

Sometimes, it can be construed that there is a national mood that seeks accountability through test scores since test scores are usually adopted as a basis for determining what needs to be corrected or changed in order to increase student's education levels. If the average test scores turn out low, there can be a lot of debate that goes on behind the scenes because the neighborhood school doesn't exceed everyone's expectations. In these instances, keep in mind that many social, environmental, linguistic and academic factors contribute to the overall assessment of testing scores.

Here are just a few things that can impact how those scores turn out. The school's turnover rate—that is the number of students who move in and out of the school during the year. In some schools the tests are being administered to students who have only been in attendance for a few weeks or even a few days. The number of students for whom English is a second language will also influence results. Test questions can easily be misunderstood if you are working in a second language and the results may not be a true measure of the student's ability. There are some teachers who complain that in addition to state mandated testing, they are required to conduct district assessments and with all the testing there is no time left to teach. Not all students enter school at the same level. Some school administrators emphasize teaching for the tests. It may be that other areas not covered by the tests are being neglected at that school. These types of instruments cannot measure many skills. Teachers change as well. The teacher who got the good or bad results in the most recent test may have moved on or retired. Add to that a margin of error, which is built into the test and you'll have to conclude test results are only one component of judging how successful a school may be. This isn't just an Arizona problem. These conditions are only elements of why testing is not an exact or full-proof indicator of what is wrong with a school or student and not a mandate against statewide testing as a whole. A school's tests results are obtained by contacting the state's Department of Education or visiting the school site and asking for the information.

WHAT TO CONSIDER

Parents moving to a new community often express concern about how to be sure their children receive the best possible education. Regardless of test scores, per pupil expenditure figures or declarations of "best school" status, your child's success or failure in school probably depends on other factors. The three most important factors in the formula for success are the child, the parents, and the teacher.

School Success Characteristics

- Student
    Readiness
    Ability
    Positive attitude
- Parents
    Positive attitude
    Value education
    Support teachers and administrators
- Teacher
    Skill
    Experience
    Enthusiasm

Visit the schools you are considering. Ask for information about:
- Staff and administrative turnover.
- Class size.
- Special programs.
- Discipline policies.

Ask to see the school handbook. Carefully study sections on discipline. Ask specific questions about drugs, drinking and violence. You'll get better information if you ask "How many incidences of students using drugs on campus occurred this year?" than if you ask, "Do you have a drug problem here?" Look for schools that encourage parental participation through organizations, advisory boards, etc. When evaluating a high school ask to see the North Central report. When possible try to talk with other families who have children in the school.

PUBLIC UNIVERSITIES

Arizona has three state universities: Arizona State University in Tempe; Northern Arizona University, in Flagstaff; and the University of Arizona in Tucson. Both ASU and the U of A are among the top research institutions in the country.

Northern Arizona University (NAU)

Northern Arizona is a multi-purpose institution with an enrollment of approximately 20,000 students. Undergraduate and graduate degrees are currently offered through six colleges and six schools. The residential campus is located at Flagstaff with instructional sites throughout the state, including an off-campus center in Yuma. The University emphasizes undergraduate programs in the arts, sciences, and professions. NAU is particularly well known as a teacher training institution and for specialized programs for Native American students, forestry, and hospitality.

University Avenue Bridge, Arizona State University.
(Courtesy of Tim Trumble)

Arizona State University (ASU)

Arizona State is a major university consisting of 12 colleges and one school. Enrollment figures show about 44,000 students. The university is largely a commuter school serving the metropolitan Phoenix area, with just over 5,000 students living on campus. The main campus is located in Tempe with several other campus locations in the metro area. The university is known for its programs in business administration, solid state electronics, the sciences, engineering, computer sciences, urban and public programs, fine arts, and law.

University Of Arizona (U OF A)

The University of Arizona is an internationally recognized leader in the fields of astronomy, optical sciences, geology, scientific instrumentation, electronics, and medicine (including cardiac care and cancer research). Current enrollment totals close to 35,000 students in its eleven colleges and eight schools. The main campus is located in Tucson.

COMMUNITY COLLEGES

An extensive community college system exists throughout the state providing opportunities for recent high-school graduates, people making a career change and those entering the job market for the first time. The ten colleges in the Maricopa Community College District are the second largest multi-college system in the nation with an enrollment of 95,000 students.

PRIVATE COLLEGES AND UNIVERSITIES

Arizona also has many excellent private colleges and universities including the internationally known American Graduate School of International Management (Thunderbird). You can gather more information about private institutions by visiting your local bookstore's reference section, searching the internet or by contacting your local public library.
For more information contact:

Phoenix Public Library
(602) 262-4636/ www.phxlib.org

Tucson Public Library
(520) 791-4393

Chapter 7
STATE GOVERNMENT

Despite a late start, Arizona matured quickly, gleaning from the experience of other states and adopting policies that have endeared it to both individuals and businesses.

EXECUTIVE

The state's administration is in the hands of the governor, secretary of state, attorney general, state treasurer, and the superintendent of public instruction. To qualify for these offices candidates must be a U.S. resident for ten years, an Arizona resident for five years and at least twenty-five years old.

A three-member Corporation Commission and a mine inspector are also elected state officials. The Corporation Commission regulates corporations within the state. The commissioners are elected to six-year terms.

LEGISLATIVE

One senator and two representatives from each of 30 legislative districts form the state legislature. There are 30 senators and 60 representatives. Legislative districts range in size from 25 square miles (a densely populated area of downtown Phoenix) to 35,000 square miles (such as one district in northern Arizona that has more canyons, mesas and rock formations than people).

A bill becomes law by passing through committees, floor debates, and chamber votes or sponsorship by lawmakers whose influence and position enable them to cut through the preliminaries. In the House, bills are assigned to three committees. The House Speaker who makes committee assignments has control over the fate of many bills.

The legislature meets about four months each year. January, February, April, and May are the heaviest working months. Floor debates are usually held on Thursdays.

To learn the current status of a bill call the House of Representatives information desk at (602) 542-4221 or the Senate information desk at (602) 542-3559.

JUDICIAL

The state supreme court has five justices, each of whom serves a six-year term. The chief justice and the vice-chief justice are elected for a five-year term by the justices. The Arizona Court of Appeals has two geographic divisions. Sessions are usually held in Tucson or Phoenix. Three-member panels hear cases that require a majority to render a decision. The governor appoints members of the state supreme court and the court of appeals.

ELECTIONS

State primary and general elections are held in even-numbered years. The governor, secretary of state, attorney general, state treasurer, and superintendent of public instruction serve four-year terms. The state senators, representatives, and state mine inspector serve two-year terms. Primaries are held in September preceding the November general election. Until recently you had to indicate a party preference at the time you registered to vote in order to vote in the primary. A proposition approved in 1998 allows Arizona voters who are registered independents or affiliated with small parties to vote in the primary election of their choice. However, if you are registered with one of the parties who have candidates fielded in the primary you cannot cross over to vote the other party's ticket.

INITIATIVE/REFERENDUM/RECALL

Statewide propositions appear on the general-election ballot. In Arizona public office holders may face a recall election if enough registered voters sign petitions indicating they want a new election. In one of the most sweeping campaign reform measures Arizona voters passed a proposition to have the public rather than lobbyists and special interests pay for state elections. Public funds are provided to candidates who agree to abide by strict limits on campaign contributions.

Arizona State Capitol Bulding, Phoenix.

PARTY POLITICS

Arizona has a presidential preference primary. During the primary elections precinct committeemen are elected to two-year terms. There are 1,947 precincts in the state. Republicans and democrats dominate state party politics. No other party has more than 1 percent of registered voters. There are slightly more republicans than democrats (about 5 percent as of January, 1999). The Republican Party has a statewide convention each year. Precinct committeemen select state and county chairman in alternating years.

> Republican State Headquarters
> 3501 N. 24th St.
> Phoenix, AZ 85016
> (602) 957-7770

Each January elected state committeemen choose the party's executive committee. County chairmen are elected for two-year terms at a countywide meeting held in late fall.

> Democratic State Headquarters
> 3109 N. 24th St Bldg. C
> Phoenix, AZ 85016
> (602) 956-1947

COUNTY GOVERNMENT

Three-member boards of supervisors, which are elected every 2 years, govern Arizona's 15 counties. The county supervisors, attorney, sheriff, treasurer, assessor, recorder, school superintendent, and clerk of the superior court serve four-year terms with elections held in even-numbered years.

The governor appoints superior court judges in Maricopa and Pima Counties. At the end of the term they run for retention in the general election. Superior court judges in other counties run in the primary and are elected in the general election to four-year terms. Justices of the peace and constables serve four-year terms.

TAXES

One reason Arizona has grown rapidly is the state's "hands off" approach to taxation. Taxation and government in general are kept to a minimum.

Property Taxes

Property taxes vary widely depending upon which taxing bodies have jurisdiction over a parcel. Cities, school districts, fire districts, and costs associated with electric districts and street improvements may be included on a tax bill.

Government bodies are restricted to a 2 percent increase per year in the amount of money that can be raised. An assessed valuation is determined, and then the property tax is calculated based on a specified percentage of the assessed valuation. Both primary and secondary taxes are levied. Primary taxes support operating expenses, while secondary taxes are collected to retire bonds and indebtedness. Arizona classifies property and imposes taxes based on the property's legal class rather than using a single assessment for all types of property. Generally speaking, the main categories are:

- Residential property, 10 percent.
- Land, 16 percent.
- Commercial property, 25 percent.

Taxes are paid in two installments. The first half is due on November 1, the second half by May 1.

A few terms that you should be familiar with when it comes to Arizona property tax include the following.

Full cash value—the current market value of the land and the improvements. Full cash value is used to compute secondary taxes for bonds, budget overrides, and special taxing districts.

Limited property value—computed by statutory formula. It cannot exceed Full Cash Value and is used to compute primary taxes for government and schools.

Real Property—includes land, buildings and other improvements on the land.

Assessed value—is determined by using the percentage listed above for each class of property.

Property taxes are computed by dividing the assessed value by 100 and then multiplying by the year's tax rate.

The following rules apply to property taxation in Arizona:

- Counties, cities, and community colleges are limited to an increase in total property tax levels of 2 percent over the previous year's levels, plus or minus the net change in construction.

- Owner-occupied residential properties are assessed at 10 percent of full cash value.

- The valuation of locally valued property is limited over the prior year's limited value. Changes in use, modifications, or destructions may affect the limitation of valuation growth.

- The state tax rate is 47¢ per $100 of assessed valuation. Other property taxes are levied locally and vary from one area to another.

- The maximum tax liability for residential property is 1 percent of limited property value, which is tied to the primary tax rate. Secondary tax rates are not limited.

Property tax exemptions are available for widows, widowers, and the disabled. Exemptions are first applied to real estate, then mobile homes, and then the individual's automobile. Contact the county assessor's office for more information on these exemptions. If you rent housing for six months or more, you may qualify for a tax credit on your Arizona state income tax return. Taxes laws are somewhat complicated, with many special considerations. For more specific information consult the Arizona Revised Statutes.

Personal Property Tax

Taxable personal property includes all assets used in the operation of a business, farm, or ranch. The minimum is set at $50 per year. This tax rate on business property has dropped by 30 percent in recent years. Businesses pay a minimum $50 tax per year. Manufactured housing is also subject to personal property tax. Arizona uses the original factory list price minus a depreciation factor based on age to determine the tax.

Sales Tax

The state imposes sales tax ranging from 3/8 to 5 percent on business activities. Retail items are taxed at 5 percent. In addition to the state tax rate, 67 municipalities impose a 1 or 2 percent tax on tax bases, which are usually narrower than state definitions. Food and pharmaceutical sales are not taxed by the state, although many cities do impose taxes on these items. A list of sales tax rates for each city can be obtained from:

> Arizona Department of Revenue
> 1600 W. Monroe St.
> Phoenix, AZ 85007
> (602) 255-3381

Estate Taxes

Overall, total impact of Arizona's estate and inheritance taxes is lower than any other state's. The actual amount will vary depending upon the amount of the net estate, personal property, and if there are adult children. If the gross estate exceeds $600,000 a return must be filed with the Arizona Department of Revenue. The state receives a portion of the tax paid to the federal government, without increasing the total tax paid on the estate. Heirs are not taxed by the state unless the proceeds qualify for federal taxation. If the federal government requires that a return be filed, you must also file an Arizona return. The Arizona return is due on the same date as the federal return.

Individual Income Taxes

All income earned or received while you are a resident (if taxable to the federal government) is taxable to Arizona with a few exceptions. Arizona does not tax federal interest, social security, or railroad retirement. All other pensions received by Arizona residents are taxed by Arizona. United States civil service, military, and Arizona state pensions are allowed a combined maximum exclusion of $2500. A credit is allowed for taxes paid to most other states on pension income. The elderly, low-income taxpayers and renters (including mobile home lots) qualify for state income tax credits. Arizona tax rates are calculated from the federal adjusted gross income figure. If you expect your Arizona gross income to be larger than $75,000 you are required to make estimated payments. You may elect to make voluntary contributions to "good causes" on your tax return. Such programs as the prevention and treatment of child abuse and Arizona wildlife benefit.

Arizona Individual Income Tax

Single and/or Married Taxpayers Filing Separately

Taxable Income

At Least	But Not Over	The Tax Is:
$0	$10,000	2.87% of taxable income
$10,001	$25,000	$287 + 3.2% of excess over $10,000
$25,001	$50,000	$767 + 3.74% of excess over $25,000
$50,001	$150,000	$1,702 + 4.72% of excess over $50,000
$150,001	and over	$6,422 + 5.04% of excess over $150,000

Married Taxpayers Filing Joint Returns and Unmarried Head of Households

Taxable Income

At Least	But Not Over	The Tax Is:
$0	$20,000	2.87% of taxable income
$20,001	$50,000	$574 + 3.20% of excess over $10,000
$50,001	$100,000	$1,534 + 3.74% of excess over $25,000
$100,001	$300,000	$3,404 + 4.72% of excess over $50,000
$300,001	and over	$12,844 + 5.04% of excess over $150,000

Source: Arizona Dept.of Revenue 2002 Tax Rate Tables

Gasoline And Motor Vehicle Taxes

Gasoline and diesel fuels are taxed by the state at 18¢ per gallon. The annual vehicle registration fee is $8.00 per vehicle ($8.25 in metro Phoenix and Tucson, including the 25¢ air quality compliance sticker); plus an air quality research fee of $1.50. Instead of personal property taxes Arizona charges a Vehicle License Tax. The initial tax base for a vehicle is computed as 60 percent of the manufacturer's list price, without options. Each year the fee is reduced by approximately 16 percent. The tax rate is calculated as $2.80 per $100 of the assessed value for new vehicles, and $2.89 per $100 of the assessed value for used vehicles.

Emissions testing is required in Maricopa and Pima Counties. Renewals are on a staggered system throughout the year, generally in the same month the plates were initially issued. License plates remain with the vehicle, and a sticker is applied to the license each year to indicate the tags are up-to-date.

Chapter 8
EVERYDAY DETAILS

There are hundreds of details newcomers need to know. Beginning with "A" for airports here are a few items you'll find of interest.

AIRPORTS

Sky Harbor International Airport in Phoenix and Tucson International Airport link Arizonans to destinations throughout the world. More than 20 million passengers pass through the Phoenix airport each year.

Good weather and clear skies have contributed to Arizona's reputation as an aviator's paradise. Close to 200 public and private airports serve the state's aviators.

AREA CODES

As with most of the rest of the country, Arizona area codes have been in the midst of change. It wasn't long ago that the whole state was served by the 602 area code. Now only the central core of the Phoenix metropolitan area uses that number. The 520 area code is for Tucson and most of the state outside of the Phoenix metro area. The 480 area code serves the East Valley including Ahwatukee and Scottsdale. The 623 area code serves the west side of Phoenix.

BICYCLES

Bicycles are accorded the same rights as other vehicles on Arizona roads. Bicyclists are required to ride as close to the right side of the road as is practical. If bicycle paths are provided, they must be used instead of the street.

When ridden at night, bicycles must have a front light, which projects a white beam 500 feet and a red rear reflector. Bicycles must also have a working brake.

Mopeds must be registered and their drivers licensed.

BOATING

The Arizona Game and Fish Department oversees the registration and regulation of boats. Every watercraft operated, moored, or anchored on the waterways of Arizona must be numbered. The owner must file an application with the Game and Fish Department and the numbers must be displayed on each side of the bow along with the current registration decal.

Under normal conditions any well-equipped and seaworthy craft with adequate freeboard may be safely used. Boaters are urged to stay alert for changing wind and weather conditions and inquire about local conditions before setting out. Children under age twelve are prohibited from driving a boat. Boat operators arrested for boating violations can be tested for drugs.

For more information contact:

Arizona Game and Fish Department
2222 W. Greenway Rd.
Phoenix, AZ 85023
(602) 942-3000

CAMPING

Campgrounds can be found in county regional parks, the state parks, and the national forest areas. City parks do not permit overnight camping. Descriptive information about more than 250 campgrounds and areas under the jurisdiction of the U.S. Forest Service, U.S. National Park Service, Bureau of Land Management, Arizona State Parks, Indian reservations and those operated by county and local governments is available from the Office of Tourism. For more information about camping contact:

Arizona Office of Tourism
(602) 230-7733 or (800) 842-8257

CHILD CARE

The Arizona Department of Health Service is responsible for licensing and inspection of child care facilities. The department publishes *A Parents Guide to Child Care*.
Copies of the guide are available by contacting:

Child Care Licensure
1647 E. Morten Ave.
Phoenix, AZ 85020
(602) 674-4340

The same agency handles day-care facility complaints. Licensing is required for home care providers with more than four children who are unrelated to the care provider. If your child is being cared for in an unlicensed home and there are complaints, the care provider may be required to close down with no advance notice. This occasionally leaves a parent scrambling for alternative care. To find someone who offers in-home childcare, check the classified ads in the local newspaper, ask for referrals from neighbors, friends, co-workers or relatives. Be sure to ask for references. Child and Family Resources maintains a roster of more than 500 certified family day-care homes. For a fee, they will find a day care home to your liking. They also offer a program which provides Sick Child Care on a temporary basis in both Phoenix and Tucson. For more information contact:

> Child and Family Resources
> 700 W. Campbell Ave. Ste. 3
> Phoenix AZ 85013
> (602) 234-3941
>
> 1030 N. Alvernon Way
> Tucson, AZ 85711
> (520) 881-8940

Child Care Resource and Referral is a non-profit agency working with family day-care homes seeking state certification. They provide training for child-care providers and attempt to match homes and day-care centers with parents' needs. Help is available for those seeking state-subsidized child care information as well. For more information contact:

> Child Care Resource and Referral
> 3910 S. Rural Rd. Ste. E
> Tempe, AZ 85282
> (480) 244-2678

Family Service Agency operates the Family Connection, which matches family child-care homes with parents. The non-profit agency conducts personal interviews with families and day-care providers and follows up on placement. The agency also does training for

childcare providers and others interested in childcare. There is a fee for this service.
For more information contact:
Family Services
1530 E. Flower St.
Phoenix, AZ 85014
(602) 264-9891

Other numbers of interest include:
Dept. of Economic Security
Day Care Home Certification
(602) 674-4220

Governor's Office for Children
(602) 542-3486

Child Protective Services
Maricopa County
(602) 506-6767
Outside Maricopa County
(800) 330-1822

Child Abuse Hotline
(888) 767-2445

Parents Anonymous
(800) 352-0528

Parents Anonymous is an excellent resource for parents interested in improving parenting skills, dealing with a crisis or seeking a support group to help with child-rearing concerns.

CHILD SUPPORT LAWS

The state's child support program services include assistance in establishing paternity for unmarried parents, locating absent parents who are not paying required support, filing court actions to set the amount of child support and collection procedures to ensure that support is paid. These services are free to any parent who has custody of a child and requests help. Request assistance from the county attorney's office where you reside. A divorced parent ordered to pay child support will automatically have the amount withheld from his or her paychecks by their employer. Unemployment insurance checks can also be garnished for child support.

Arizona cooperates with other state and the federal government agencies in tracking parents who do not support their children.

CITY DRIVING

The street system in metropolitan Phoenix is based on a grid with major intersections at one-mile intervals. Only a few streets such as Grand Avenue and Cave Creek Road diverge from the grid. Otherwise it's straight sailing except for the city mountains. A few streets end abruptly near the mountains and pick up again on the other side. Plan your route with that in mind. Seventh Street, Cave Creek Boulevard and the Squaw Peak Parkway (AZ 51) are all mountain pass streets through the North Phoenix Mountain Preserves. You can take 44th Street, 64th Street (Invergordon Rd.) or Scottsdale Road to get around Camelback Mountain. Interstate 10 is the major route around South Mountain.

In Phoenix, zero point is the intersection of Central Avenue and Washington Street. East of Central Avenue, the north and south thoroughfares are called streets, and west of Central Avenue, avenues. Both are numbered outward from Central. For example,

First Street and First Avenue each lie one block out from Central. North and south designations begin at Washington Street. Crosstown streets have names and are designated East or West (again from Central Avenue). In general, Scottsdale streets conform to the Phoenix system. Thus, the intersection of Scottsdale Road and Lincoln Drive is 7200 East and 6500 North. Zero point in Tempe is at Mill Avenue and the Salt River. In Mesa, streets are numbered from Center and Main Streets. Tempe and Mesa name most streets, rather than using the north/south number names you'll find in Phoenix and Scottsdale.

Reverse lanes are in operation on some streets to help the weekday flow of rush hour traffic. In the morning the center lanes on Seventh Street and Seventh Avenue in Phoenix carry traffic into the city (south), and in the evening rush hour traffic flows out of the city (north) in the same lane. At other non-rush times and on weekends, the lane is used for left turns. Reverse lanes are in operation from 6 a.m. to 9 a.m. and 4 p.m. to 6 p.m.; Monday through Friday, excluding holidays. Although the lanes are marked with traffic signs, the best advice is to avoid the center lane until you are sure you know which direction traffic is flowing.

In Tucson, zero point is the intersection of Broadway and Stone. Interstate 10 is a major north-south cross route, along with Oracle Road and First, Euclid and Campbell Avenues. The major east-west routes are Speedway Boulevard, Broadway, and 22nd Street. Kino Boulevard connects the University of Arizona and Tucson International Airport on the south side.

Reversible lanes are on East Grant Road, East Speedway Boulevard, East Fifth and Sixth Streets and East Broadway.

Right turns can be made at red lights if traffic is clear and no prohibiting sign has been posted. This also applies to left turns made from a one-way street onto another one-way street.

COMMUNITY PROPERTY

As a community property state, real or personal property acquired by either husband or wife during a marriage may be considered community property of both. As a general rule, property acquired before a marriage and property acquired by one spouse by gift or inheritance is considered separate property. Virtually everything else acquired during a marriage is community property.

An important exception exists for joint tenancy property, on the death of one joint tenant the property passes to the remaining joint tenant. If you are moving from a state that does not have a community property law, check to be sure that your will conforms to Arizona laws. (Also see divorce.)

DEW POINT

The dew point is the temperature at which water can condense in the atmosphere. Some homes use evaporative coolers or "swamp boxes" to blow moisture into a room. They may be used in addition to air conditioners or may be the home's only cooling system. They are not as effective, however, once the dew point reaches 55 degrees and the air is saturated with moisture. The dew point varies with the temperature, but not to the same extent as relative humidity. Dew point readings are generally included in Arizona weather reports.

DIVORCE

Arizona is a no-fault divorce state. Community property laws affect divorce settlements. In fixing the amount and duration of alimony the court considers the contribution one spouse made to the earning ability of the other, as well as any income or career sacrifices a spouse may have made for the other's benefit. The court also considers the ability of both parties to contribute to the costs of educating their children. They also give weight to marriages of long duration if a spouse's age might prevent finding suitable employment after the divorce or legal separation. (Also see Community Property.) Parents of minor children are required to attend an education class geared toward avoiding conflict over child-related issues.

DRIVER'S LICENSES

Who Needs an Arizona Driver's License?

All residents must have an Arizona driver's license to operate a vehicle on the streets or highways of Arizona. State law requires the following individuals obtain an Arizona license:

- Anyone who lives in the state for seven months or more during a calendar year.
- Anyone who is employed in the state other than seasonal agricultural work or temporary work lasting less than three months.
- Anyone who has children in a public school and does not pay non-resident tuition.
- Anyone who says they are a resident to obtain resident rates at any public school or to obtain a state license.
- Out-of-state students are not considered residents even if they are enrolled for more than seven hours, even if they are employed.

New Residents

New residents are expected to obtain an Arizona driver's license as soon as they arrive. There is no grace period. Out-of-state applicants who do not have a valid driver's license must prove they are still eligible to have a license from the last state in which they were licensed. Arizona uses the National Driver Registry, a nationwide computer system that shows problem drivers to determine if false information is being submitted or if there are any outstanding warrants or other unresolved actions in another state. The Driver's License Compact Law requires surrender of out-of-state licenses when applying for an Arizona license. Your first Arizona driver's license will not expire until you are 60. You will be required to update your photo and take an eye test every 12 years. Drivers fifty-five years' and older will receive a five-year license. Fees for the license vary according to the length of time in which it is issued.

Applying For A License

When applying you must bring three forms of identification, one of which includes your picture. If you are licensed in another state you must bring in your out-of-state driver license and one other form of identification, take the vision test and pay the fee. A written test is not required. A driving test is required if your license has been canceled 1 year or more, expired 1 year or more, revoked, or you are applying for a new license and do not have a current license from another state.

If you are under eighteen you must have the signature of at least one responsible adult (parent/guardian). That adult may later cancel the minor's license by submitting an affidavit to the Motor Vehicle Division if they change their mind about being responsible for the driver.

You'll be required to take a written test, a vision test, and have your photo taken. New drivers must also pass a road test. The Arizona Driver's License Manual provides all the information you need to pass the written test. Manuals are available at examination stations. You must be sixteen years old in order to apply for a driver's license. Instruction permits are issued to applicants who are at least fifteen years and seven months old. No refunds are made on any fees. If you fail the required tests you have six months or three attempts (whichever comes first) to pass. For information about stations, contact the Motor Vehicle Division of the Arizona Department of Transportation: (602) 255-0072.

Non-driver Identification Cards

Non-drivers may apply for a permanent identification card at any Driver's License Examining Station. There is a one-time $12 fee for these cards, which are useful when cashing checks or applying for services. The fee may be waived if you are over sixty-five years old or are disabled.

Driving While Intoxicated

A blood alcohol content of .10 percent is evidence that you are driving while under the influence of alcohol. In some cases a driver may be found guilty with less than a .10 test result. If you are under twenty-one you are considered impaired if there is any alcohol concentration in your blood. If you refuse to take a breath, blood or urine test, the penalty is a one-year suspension of driving privileges. Even if the Driving Under the Influence(DUI) charges are dismissed, your license may be suspended for refusal to take the test.

Police may seize the driver's license of a motorist suspected of driving drunk and issue a 15-day driving permit, giving the driver time to appeal. Motorists who refuse to take a blood or urine test for drugs may also lose their licenses.

Drivers convicted for the first time face mandatory penalties of 10 days in jail, a fine of at least $250 and a 90-day license suspension. A second offense brings a 90-day jail sentence, a $500 fine, and a year's suspension of the driver's license. Aggravated DUI nets a four-year sentence and a three-year license revocation.

The state may seize vehicles of repeat offenders. Your vehicle may also be seized if you are convicted of driving while under the influence of alcohol or drugs while your license has been suspended, cancelled, or revoked.

Medical Conditions

A space is provided on Arizona driver's licenses to note medical conditions. To place a notation on the license, a signed statement from a licensed physician is needed.

Organ Donors

You may indicate on your driver's license if you wish to participate in the Anatomical Gift Act. This permission can be revoked at any time by signing the back of the license.

Name and Address Changes

You are required by law to notify the Motor Vehicle Department in writing within 10 days if you change your name or address. If you want an updated license, you must pay an additional fee.

DRUGS

Possession of the smallest usable amount of marijuana nets a $750 fine. In addition to the fine, a minimum mandatory 24 hours of community service is required and a jail sentence is also possible. Depending on the circumstances, possession of marijuana could easily be a felony with a minimum $2,000 fine and imprisonment of up to 5 years. Offenses occurring near school grounds involving larger quantities, or dangerous or narcotic drugs, net even stiffer penalties. One county attorney advises, "Don't get caught with illegal drugs in Arizona."

FIREARMS

Arizona's gun law allows anyone who has no felony record or history of mental illness to buy a gun and wear it in view. Shop owners may prohibit entrance or require you to check your weapon at the entrance. Pistols and rifles must be carried openly, while only pocketknives may be carried concealed. Concealed weapons may be carried with a special permit, which requires attending an instructional program. You must be over twenty-one and have had sixteen hours of firearms training. Sawed-off shotguns and automatic weapons are prohibited. Other laws prohibit minors from carrying guns without a parent's notarized permission statement. For more information you may obtain a copy of *Arizona Gun Laws* at your local book store.

FINDING AN ACCOUNTANT

The Arizona Society of Certified Public Accountants operates a referral service, which will refer you to a CPA in your area by

specialty. For more information contact:
>   The Arizona Society of CPAs
>   (602) 252-4144 x 200

FINDING A DENTIST

The Arizona Dental Association makes referrals to its members. Callers are given the names of three dentists in their area to choose from. For more information contact:
>   Arizona Dental Association
>   (602) 957-4864

FINDING A DOCTOR

There are many physicians to select from in Phoenix and Tucson. Referrals are made by the county medical societies. When you contact either association, you receive the name of a member in your area with the specialty you are seeking. For more information contact:
>   Maricopa County M.D. Referral
>   (602) 252-2844
>   Pima County M.D. Referral
>   (520) 795-7985

In addition, many hospitals make referrals to doctors on their staffs. The Board of Medical Examiners and the Board of Osteopathic Examiners investigates complaints and compiles records on Arizona physicians. Files are available for public inspection. You may write or visit the offices to obtain background information, licensing, letters of concern, and stipulations.

FINDING A LAWYER

The Maricopa County Bar Association operates the Lawyer Referral Service in Phoenix. Half-hour consultations can be scheduled by calling (602) 257-4434. In Pima County, contact Lawyer Referral Service by calling (520) 623-4625.

You can also call the State Bar at (602) 340-7300 for lists of certified specialists in areas such as bankruptcy, criminal law, estates and trusts, family law, injury and wrongful death, real estate and tax or worker's compensation.

Nearly every courthouse in Arizona has a computerized self-service center for individuals representing themselves. Simple on-screen instructions allow you to complete divorce and other court papers for filing. Instructions forms and assistance for a variety of legal procedures can be accessed as well as a list of lawyers willing to advise people who would like to represent themselves. For more information contact the clerk of the county superior court.

The Arizona Modest Means Panel is a source of assistance for individuals who make too much money to qualify for free legal service, but still need help with legal issues. For more information: (602) 266-2322.

Ethical complaints about lawyers may be filed with the State Bar Association. For more information:

Commission on Judicial Conduct
1501 W. Washington St. Ste. 229
Phoenix, AZ 85007
(602) 340-7280

FINDING A MECHANIC

The Arizona Automobile Association makes free referrals to car-repair service establishments that have AAA approval. For more

information call one of these numbers:
>   Phoenix Area
>   (602) 274-1116
>   Outside the Phoenix metro area:
>   (800) 352-5382

GOLF

Arizona has long been a golfer's paradise. The year-round season has made the state a favorite of duffers and pros alike. You'll find traditional as well as the challenging desert courses here, several of which are considered among the nation's premiere courses. The Arizona Golf Association publishes a directory of golf courses, which gives detailed information on more than 250 courses in the state. Call for current price information.

>   Arizona Golf Association
>   (602) 944-3035

Phoenician Golf Course. The Phoenician Resort, Scottsdale.
(Courtesy of Debs Metzong)

HOMESTEAD EXEMPTION

Up to $100,000 in home equity is protected from most creditors and lawsuits. You are no longer required to record a homestead declaration in order to protect your home.

HUNTING AND FISHING

Anyone over the age of fourteen is required to have a license to fish in the state. Trout fishing requires the purchase of an additional stamp. Residents may obtain fishing regulations at outlets where licenses are sold, and non-residents may obtain regulations by writing to the Game and Fish Department.

Anyone fourteen years old or older may hunt wildlife in Arizona with a hunting license. No state license, tag, or permit is required to hunt or fish on any Indian reservation in this state, however, reservation restrictions do apply. Hunting regulations are complex and vary considerably by game and locale.

Land in Arizona is owned or managed by five different governments or agencies and each has its own access rules. Generally U.S. Forest Service, Bureau of Land Management, and State of Arizona lands are open for hunting. National parks, national monuments, and some state parks are not.

The Arizona Game and Fish Department, which is funded through license fees and permit tags, oversees hunting and fishing in the state. For more information:

Arizona Game and Fish Department
(602) 942-3000
In Tucson call: (520) 628-5376

IMMIGRATION

U.S. Department of Immigration and Naturalization offices are located at:

2035 N. Central Ave.
Phoenix, AZ 85004
(602) 379-3122

6431 S. Country Club Rd.
Tucson, AZ 85706
(520) 670-4624

INFORMATION AND REFERRAL

Information and Referral to social service agencies are available in Phoenix by calling (602) 263-8856 and in Tucson by calling (520) 881-1794.

INSURANCE

The state of Arizona publishes premium surveys based on typical transactions for auto and homeowner's insurance. Rates vary considerably between companies. The message is: shop around for the policy that will best suit your needs. Complaint records are also available from the Insurance Department. Over 2500 insurance companies are licensed to do business in the state of Arizona. To obtain the automobile or homeowners premium survey, send a

business-size self-addressed stamped envelope to:
State Department of Insurance
2910 N. 44th St. Ste. 210
Phoenix, AZ 85018
(602) 912-8444

400 W. Congress St.
Tucson, AZ 85701
(520) 628-6370

LEMON LAW

A "lemon law" provides new car buyers additional protection against perpetually defective cars. It entitles new car owners to either a comparable new car or cash refund if:

- the dealer is unable to get a problem repaired in four attempts within the first year of ownership or during the express warranty period (whichever is shorter).

- the car is out of service for repair work for 30 days or more within the first year of warranty period, whichever is sooner.

For the defect to be covered by this law, it must substantially impair the use and value of the car and be covered by an express warranty. The defect may not be the result of abuse, neglect, or unauthorized modification or alteration.

Used cars sold by dealers are now covered by similar legislation. The car must be driveable for at least 15 days or 500 miles after it is purchased. If the car breaks down during that time, the dealer must either repair it or refund the buyer's money.

LIQUOR

To purchase, serve or consume alcoholic beverages in the state you must be twenty-one years of age or older. Alcohol may not be consumed in a vehicle or in an original container in public areas. Liquor is not sold between 1 a.m. and 7 a.m. Monday through Saturday or between 1 a.m. and 10 a.m. on Sunday. The legal limit is .10 Blood Alcohol Concentration, although you can be arrested at a lower limit if you are impaired.

LOTTERY

Arizona has several lottery games. About 50 percent of lottery proceeds are returned to the players as winnings. The rest, less operating expenses, is used for improving transportation, education, parks, building and economic development. Tickets are sold at a variety of retail outlets. Drawings are held on Wednesday and Saturday evenings.

Lotto ticket purchasers select six numbers. If no one has picked all six winning numbers for the week, the jackpot accumulates to the following drawing. If more than one person picks all six numbers, the winnings are shared. The jackpot is often $1 million or more. Numbers can be selected individually or the computer will randomly select your numbers in a "quick pick." There are also instant "scratch off" games and games with smaller prizes and more frequent drawings. Most winners of large prizes have the option of choosing an annuity paid over 20 years or taking a smaller lump sum payment.

Arizona participates in the multi-state Powerball lottery. Drawings are held every Wednesday and Saturday with a guaranteed $10 million jackpot.

MANDATORY INSURANCE

Arizona's mandatory insurance law requires that all vehicle owners carry $40,000 liability insurance ($15,000 injury to one person, $30,000 injury to two or more persons, and $10,000 property damage). The vehicle owner must maintain evidence of financial responsibility in the vehicle at all times. You can meet this requirement by having one of the following items in your car:

- A standard liability policy.
- A photocopy of a liability policy.
- A Certificate of Insurance.
- A copy of a $40,000 Surety Bond.
- A copy of a $40,000 Certificate of Deposit filed with the State Treasurer, or
- A vehicle identification card issued by an insurance company.

Penalties for not carrying adequate insurance range from fines of $250-750, suspension of driver's license and vehicle registration from 90 days to 1 year and, in some cases, a jail sentence.

You must notify the Motor Vehicle Division within 10 days if you change your policy number, insurance company, or the vehicle covered on your liability insurance policy. Your vehicle registration and plates may be suspended if you fail to report these changes.

MARRIAGE

Getting married is a simple procedure in the state if you are twenty-two or older. No blood test or waiting period is required. Copies of divorce papers are not required. Licenses can be obtained from the clerk of the superior court, the justice courts, or city hall through the county where the marriage will be performed. The fee is $50 and is valid for 1 year. If you are eighteen to twenty-two years old you must provide proof of your age with either a birth certificate or a valid driver's license. In addition sixteen and seventeen year-olds must have parental consent. Anyone under sixteen must also have a court order permitting the marriage. For those wishing to make a more binding commitment, covenant marriages are an option. Premarital counseling is required and divorce is more difficult. For information on covenant marriages contact the Arizona Office of the Courts.

MEDICAL CARE

The state has many state-of-the-art medical facilities. The University of Arizona in Tucson is a leader in the fields of cancer research, heart surgery, and integrated healing. Telemedicine links rural communities to specialists at the university. In Phoenix, Barrow Neurological Institute, which is associated with St. Joseph's Medical Center, is a leader in neuroscience research and treatment and includes the Muhammad Ali Parkinson's Research Center. Good Samaritan Medical Center in Phoenix, St. Joseph's Hospital in Phoenix, and Tucson's University Medical Center each have more than 600 beds. The Mayo Clinic operates facilities in Scottsdale.

The Arizona Health Care Cost Containment System (AHCCCS) is Arizona's Medicaid program and the state's health care program for those who do not qualify for Medicaid. About 10 percent of the state's population are served by AHCCCS. (The letters AHCCCS are pronounced as though they were spelled access.) More than three times as many children as adults receive assistance. Most participants receive care through managed health care plans. The AHCCCS system was started in 1982 and after a number of rocky years has evolved into a model for other states. The Arizona Long Term Care System provides assistance for the developmentally disabled, the elderly and physically disabled. KidsCare provides medical care for children under age nineteen whose family income is less than 150% of the federal poverty level. Both are programs overseen by AHCCCS.

MILEPOSTS

To make getting around just a bit easier, you'll find that Arizona has highway reference markers. The markers can be found two feet from the road's right shoulder and are a mile apart.

If you have an accident, mechanical problem, run out of gas, or are unable to proceed, use the nearest milepost to determine your exact location. They are also handy for giving directions to someone you are planning to meet, finding trailheads, etc.

If you get into trouble, the Division of Motor Vehicles recommends you note the number of the route you are traveling, your direction, and approximate distance to the next milepost, then use the most accessible means of communication to relay your message to the Department of Public Safety.

MONEY MATTERS

Merchants are not required by law to accept checks. You are most likely to encounter difficulty cashing out-of-state checks, those with low check numbers, or those that are not preprinted. Many merchants require an Arizona driver's license or non-driver's identification card.

It is a misdemeanor to write a bad check in Arizona. If you do not respond in 12 days to someone's request to make good on a check the bank has returned, the county attorney may prosecute.

Bad check writers face a jail sentence, fines and are required to pay restitution.

In some cases the county attorney may offer a chance to pay restitution and statutory fees to have the charges dropped. In Maricopa County, to qualify, you must have no previous bad check charges or other pending criminal charges. It must not be an excessively large check, and no reason to suggest intent to defraud.

PASSPORT OFFICES

To apply for a passport you must show proof of U.S. citizenship, such as a certified copy of a birth certificate or an original copy of a naturalization certificate, and a valid driver's license or passport photo. Additional information about passports is available by calling the court clerk passport agent at (602) 506-3369 in Phoenix or (520) 740-8333 in Tucson. One-day passport service is not available in Arizona.

PROFESSIONAL SPORTS

The NBA's Phoenix Suns take on challengers at America West Arena in Phoenix. For a schedule and ticket information, call (602) 379-7867. From June through August the WNBA Phoenix Mercury play at the same location. For information call (602) 252-9622.

For the NFL's Arizona Cardinals schedule and ticket information, call (602) 379-0102.

The NHL Phoenix Coyotes have been playing in Phoenix since 1996 when they left Winnipeg. For ticket information call (602) 379-7800.

The National League Arizona Diamondbacks play at Bank One Ballpark in Phoenix. For more information call (888) 777-4664.

Each spring Arizonans get a preview of the national pastime as the Cactus League gears up for a month of spring training. In the preseason all seats are up close with plenty of opportunity to catch a fly ball or secure an autograph. Teams training in Arizona include: the Anaheim Angels, Chicago Cubs, Arizona Diamondbacks, Oakland A's, San Francisco Giants, Milwaukee Brewers, and the Seattle Mariners.

Several professional golf tournaments are held in the state each year. The tournaments change names depending on corporate sponsors. Phoenix hosts a PGA, LPGA and Seniors Tournament and Tucson hosts a PGA tourney.

Tennis superstars regularly swing into action with major national junior, senior, and pro tournaments each season as well as frequent charitable exhibitions by pro players.

PETS

All dogs more than four months old coming into the state must be vaccinated and licensed within 30 days of entry. Cats do not have to be vaccinated or licensed. To obtain a dog license, you must have a valid rabies vaccination certificate for your animal. If your pet has been vaccinated in another state within the last 3 years, obtain a certificate from your vet before you move. Each county handles pet licensing.

Most cities and towns have laws requiring dogs be on a leash, even when they are on the owner's private property. Some counties also have leash laws.

It is especially hazardous to leave animals inside a car during the warm months. Temperatures reach dangerous levels in minutes. Leaving the windows open slightly is not adequate. When the mercury begins to climb, your pet will be much safer left at home.

PUBLIC TRANSIT

Transit systems throughout the Phoenix area are linked by a regional transportation system. Regular fares are $1.25. Children under six are free. Express routes are $1.75. Special services are available for handicapped, hearing impaired, and elderly riders. Discount fares are available for youth six through eighteen, those sixty-five and older and those with disabilities. In many areas door-to-door Dial-A-Ride service is available. Dial-a-Ride fares vary, based upon the distance traveled. For more information on routes, services, or fares phone (602) 253-5000. The Bus Book with schedules and other information is available from the bus driver, the library or the transit authority. DASH, is a free Downtown Area Shuttle that operates between the downtown Phoenix area and the Capitol. A similar service, FLASH, operates from ASU in downtown Tempe to the Phoenix zoo.

In Tucson, Sun Tran provides public bus service. Regular fares are $1.00. Children five and under ride for free, and seniors and disabled fares are 40¢. Call (520) 792-9222 for schedule and route information.

RIGHT TO DIE

Patients in Arizona have a legal right to refuse treatment, even if their decision results in death. The state supreme court has ruled that patients do not lose the right to refuse treatment if they are unable to act on their own. A court-appointed guardian can act, based on such things as a Living Will or a patient's "best interests." Suffering, the quality of life, and how long a person could be expected to live are considered in determining a patient's best interests.

School Zones

The posted speed limit approaching a school crossing never exceeds 15 mph. Police officers will issue civil traffic citations to drivers who exceed the 15 mph speed limit.

The law requires reduced speed only while "approaching a school crossing." As long as it can be done safely, a driver may return to normal speed immediately after passing the crossing.

Regardless of the number of lanes in each direction, drivers also must observe the "no passing" rule in school zones. In other words, the slowest car controls the speed.

When approaching a stopped school bus with flashing lights and an extended "stop" sign, drivers are required to come to a full stop and remain stopped until the signals are withdrawn or the bus begins to move again. The requirement to stop applies to vehicles moving in either direction on the roadway, not just to those behind the bus.

Seat Belt Laws

Drivers and front seat passengers in cars built after 1972 must wear seat belts. Children under age five and those weighing less than 40 pounds must be secured in child passenger restraints. Parents who don't comply can be fined.

Take special care in the summer before buckling up your child. Seat belts can be "hot enough to burn." Carry a small spray bottle of water with you. A quick spray will help cool the hot metal fasteners.

Skiing

City dwellers can be on the slopes in a matter of hours. Arizona has four major snow ski areas in the state. The southern-most ski area in the United States is at Mount Lemmon in the Catalina Mountains, just an hour's drive from Tucson. In northern Arizona you'll find Snowbowl, Bill Williams Mountain and Sunrise. Sunrise is owned and operated by the White Mountain Apache Tribe. Cross-country skiing is plentiful in the north with popular trails near Mormon Lake, Greer, and Springerville.

SMALL CLAIMS COURT

The Small Claims Division of the justice courts was created so people could present a claim in court without having to use a lawyer. Lawyers are not permitted to represent parties in the Small Claims Division unless both sides agree.

Most claims, which do not exceed $2,500, can be filed in the Small Claims Division. Simple forms are available and filing fees are minimal. A court hearing is generally scheduled within 60 days. At that time both sides may present witnesses and documents to support their case. The judge makes a decision within 10 days.

One difficulty may be in collecting on the judgment. The court says only that the money is owed, it does not establish repayment, and you're on your own to collect. However, if the defendant fails to pay, you can notify the credit bureau and the default will become a part of the defendant's credit rating.

Justice courts handle matters up to $10,000. Justice courts generally take only a month or two to hear cases. There are less stringent rules and the matter can often be handled without an attorney. Matters involving sums over $10,000 must go to superior court.

SMOKING

Several major Arizona cities, including Phoenix. Mesa, Tempe, Scottsdale, and Tucson restrict smoking in public places. Employees may be required to smoke only in designated areas. Large restaurants must also provide space for non-smokers. At the state Capitol smoking is banned in most state buildings.

SOCIAL SECURITY

Information about Social Security benefits can be obtained by contacting offices located in Flagstaff, Glendale, Mesa, Tucson, Phoenix, and Scottsdale. For information and assistance phone (800) 772-1213.

SOUTH OF THE BORDER

There are six border crossings between the 230-mile Arizona-Mexico dividing line, the most popular of which is Nogales, just 63 miles south of Tucson.

American citizens do not need visas to visit a border community if you do not plan to travel more than 3 miles below the border or stay more than 72 hours. You can also park your car and walk across the border. If you are going farther or are planning an extended stay, you will need a tourist card and an automobile permit. You'll also need identification such as a birth certificate, voter's registration card, passport or military identification card that shows your place of birth, or a typewritten notarized affidavit showing your name, place of birth, and citizenship is required. Automobile permits are required if you are driving a distance into Mexico. To obtain the permit you may be required to place a bond assuring that you will return with the car (the bond may be as much as $1000). This is done to prevent circumventing the import tax on vehicles which will be staying in Mexico. You can use a credit card or cash to place the bond. It is returned to you when you return with the vehicle. Most U.S. auto insurance policies do not cover driving in Mexico. Mexican auto insurance can be obtained near the border or may be available from your motor club.

Tourist cards are available at the border or at:

Mexican Consulate

553 S. Stone Ave.

Tucson, AZ 85701

(520) 882-5595

In Nogales, the Calle Obregon is the main shopping area, but you'll also be pleased with the Calle Elias near the Morley Street border crossing, just east of the gate.

Serapes, pottery, leather wallets, guitars, as well as vanilla, Tequila, Kahlua, and Mexican rum and brandy are often on Arizonans' shopping lists.

While the peso is standard currency, you'll have no trouble paying in American dollars near the border. You can bring $400 of merchandise back into the United States duty-free. Only one quart of liquor per adult can be brought back.

SPEED LIMITS

Arizona speed limits to remember are:
- 15 miles per hour when approaching a school crossing.
- 25 miles per hour when in any business or residential district.
- 55 miles per hour in most other locations.
- 65 miles per hour on most rural interstates (only if posted).

TIME ZONES

Unlike the rest of the nation, Arizona never turns the clock back or ahead. The state is on Mountain Standard Time all year. The only exception is the Navajo nation, which observes daylight savings time.

TINTED AUTOMOBILE WINDOWS

Arizonans have found innovative ways to deal with the summer sun, but safety comes first. Dark film and tinted windows may help keep your auto cool in the summer; however, the law prohibits restricting visibility. Vehicle window film or screening that blocks more than 33 percent of the light or reflects more than 35 percent is illegal. The law applies to the driver side window and the front passenger side window.

The windshield can have a strip of film about six inches across the top. A violation is a misdemeanor and carries a maximum sentence of 30 days in jail.

VEHICLE REGISTRATION

Arizona law very clearly requires that new residents register their vehicles. There is a stiff fine ($300) if you fail to do so. A non-resident must register a motor vehicle in Arizona upon establishing residency, accepting employment, enrolling children in a public school, or staying in the state for seven months or more during the year.

Application for registration and title is made with the County Assessor. Residents of Maricopa and Pima Counties must obtain an Emissions Compliance form from an emissions testing station before applying for registration.

You will be required to:
- Turn in your out-of-state plates.
- Furnish your previous registration card.
- Obtain a Level 1 inspection slip from an MVD auto license office.
- Present the previous title, if from a title state.
- Prove lien clearance, if applicable.
- Show a notarized bill of sale, if from a non-title state, and official verification that no lien exists against the vehicle.

Personalized plates are available for an initial fee of $25 plus $25 per year, in addition to the regular costs of plates and registration.

Handicapped License Plates

Forms for obtaining handicapped auto license plates are available from the county license plate departments. A licensed Arizona physician must state in writing that the applicant meets two of the following six criteria:
- Is physically unable to make use of the public bus or train.
- Is physically unable to perform sustained work activity for more than six hours.
- Has pronounced disfigurement or deformity.
- Is physically unable to climb one flight of stairs or walk 50 yards on the level without pause.
- Has significant loss of manual dexterity or coordination which severely restricts performance of major life activities.

Permits are available from the State Motor Vehicle Division for temporary disabilities. It is a misdemeanor for an able-bodied person to park in spaces designated for the handicapped.

Emissions Testing

All vehicles manufactured since 1967, including diesels, must be emissions-inspected before registration if you live in Maricopa or Pima County. All gas-powered vehicles of model year 1975 or newer are checked to make sure that factory-installed emissions devices have not been removed, defeated, or altered. Some vehicles are not required to have emissions tests. They include electric-powered vehicles, golf carts, new vehicles at the time of the first sale, vehicles with engines of less than 90 cc, and diesel-powered vehicles.

Emissions testing requirements vary slightly between Maricopa and Pima Counties. Some newer vehicles are eligible for alternate year testing. For more specific information, phone (800) 284-7748. You are also required to meet emissions standards if you live elsewhere, but work in Maricopa or Pima Counties.

VETERANS' ASSISTANCE

There are three VA hospitals in Arizona, a regional VA office in Phoenix, and many active veterans' organizations. A statewide toll-free number, (800) 827-1000, can put you in touch with the one you need. VA Medical Centers are located in Phoenix, Tucson, and Prescott.

VOTER REGISTRATION

Registering to vote in Arizona is easy. Mail-in forms are available or you can register at any driver's license station. The U.S. post offices, city or town clerks, some banks and grocery stores, and many libraries also have the forms.

To vote in an Arizona election you must:
- Be a citizen of the United States.
- Be at least eighteen years old on election day.
- Have resided in the state 29 days prior to the election.
- Be able to write your own name or make your own mark (unless physically disabled).
- Never have been convicted of treason or a felony unless civil rights have been restored.
- Not be insane, or under guardianship.

You are no longer required to specify your political party affiliation at the time you register if you plan to vote in primary elections. Independents and those affiliated with small parties may specify their choice of party on the day of the primary.

For most elections registration is required 29 days before the election. Voters who do not cast ballots in the general election may be removed from voter registration rolls.

WILLS

Any person who is at least eighteen years old and of sound mind can write a will in Arizona. Handwritten wills are valid. Provisions detailing who is to receive your property must also be in your writing. Wills prepared in other states are valid in Arizona. You may select a personal representative or executor from out-of-state, although it is not recommended. Wills other than those handwritten must be witnessed by two disinterested adults.

(Also see Community Property.)

Chapter 9
KEEPING YOUR COOL

SKIN PROTECTION

In Arizona, the sun is a mixed blessing. While it provides relief from aching joints, psoriasis, acne, and supplies Vitamin D, it can also cause wrinkling, premature aging of the skin, leathery and rough skin, sunburn, and skin cancer.

Everyone in Arizona is at high risk for developing skin cancer due to the sun's high intensity, latitude, altitude, and clear skies. Arizona has the highest rate of skin cancer in the United States, although more than 95 percent of such cancers can be prevented.

The Arizona Sun Awareness Center at the University of Arizona recommends that you:

• Use a sunscreen with a high Sun Protection Factor. SPF 15 generally gives adequate protection. SPF 15 will protect most people even in summer for about two-and-a-half hours. Products are now available with very high SPF numbers and water resistance, which can provide daylong protection. Apply sunscreen 30 minutes before going out. The screening agent needs time to react with your skin. Reapply sunscreen if you are out for a long time or if your sunscreen may have washed off. The ultraviolet (UV) portion of sunlight, which is the leading cause of skin cancer, cannot be seen or felt. It gets to your skin even on cloudy days and under water. UV rays bounce off water, tile, cement, sand, and snow. You need sunscreen even if you wear a hat, use a golfcart, carry an umbrella, or stand under a tree. Be sure to protect your ears, the backs of your neck, throat, hands, tops of feet and bald spots.

- Avoid the sun between 10 a.m. and 3 p.m. when the sun's rays are strongest. Work or play outdoors earlier or later, whenever you can.

- In addition to applying sunscreen, cover up. Wear long sleeves, long pants, wide brimmed hats, and protective sunglasses that screen out ultraviolet light.

- Know your skin moles and see a doctor when they change. Light-colored, lightweight clothing, which reflects heat and light, is your best choice. Natural fibers, such as cotton and linen, cool better than polyesters. A hat with a wide brim will protect both your eyes and neck. The best choice is a light-colored straw hat with holes for ventilation.

- Certain drugs may cause your skin to be particularly sensitive to the sun's ultraviolet rays, including:
    - Some antibiotics, such as tetracycline.
    - Some diuretics (water pills).
    - Some tranquilizers, such as Thorazine and Stelazine.
    - Sulfa drugs.
    - Some birth control pills and hormones.

This same type of photosensitivity may develop from the use of certain perfumes and artificial sweeteners as well as some cosmetics. Check with your pharmacist or physician to see if any of the medications you take are affected by exposure to the sun. Keep in mind that children's tender skin may burn more rapidly than an adult's might.

MANAGING THE HEAT

"Desert sunshine" is different from sunlight in other areas of the country. First of all, there's much more of it. The clear desert air and light-reflective terrain combine to deliver a more intense dose of sun to your skin than in many other parts of the country. Desert temperatures are hotter and your body begins soaking up heat from the air at 92 degrees. Body temperature will also increase from heat reflected from the ground, direct contact with heated objects, and any work or exercise. Dangerous elevations of body temperature can be caused by absorbing too much heat or by generating it. In the desert, the chances of a person's body reaching dangerous temperature levels must be considered. An elevation of six to eight degrees above the normal for any extended length of time can be fatal.

Dehydration

Your body's major means of cooling itself is by sweating. It is vital that the fluid lost in this way be replaced. Dehydration is a sign that body fluids are being lost. The symptoms include thirst, a tired, lazy feeling, slower body movements, loss of appetite, dizziness, and dry mouth. These are warning signs to drink more water. It is important to begin replacing fluids before symptoms appear. Water is an effective thirst quencher, better than soda, milk, or fruit juice. Warm or cool water is better than ice cold water. Smoking and alcohol consumption also hasten dehydration.

Symptoms of overheating are serious and call for prompt attention. While heatstroke is more severe than exhaustion, both problems indicate that the victim should be promptly removed from the sunlight and medical attention sought.

Heat Exhaustion

Moist, pale, cool skin, muscle cramps and weakness and a weak pulse are signs of heat exhaustion.

Heatstroke

Headache, nausea, dry, red and hot skin; strong, fast pulse; convulsions; and unconsciousness are signs of heatstroke. They are signs that the body's cooling system has broken down completely. Get out of the sun and get help quickly.

When temperatures are on the rise, slow down. Pay attention to your body's early warning signs and head for the shade at the first sign of overheating. In very hot weather, cut back on food consumption. Eating increases your body heat and contributes to water loss. Drink plenty of water. In the summer months it's a good idea to keep a supply of drinking water in your car.

Gradual temperature change is better than sudden changes. Shorten the time you are exposed to the heat and watch out for sunburns.

DESERT SURVIVAL

Arizonans are creative in their attempts to cool off. Some of their solutions to the heat are just common sense. Here are a few tips.

Put on a hat to give yourself some portable shade. If it's really hot, you can wet a bandana and drape it under the hat and you'll have your own evaporative cooling system. This isn't the most sophisticated look, but it works. Sunglasses will slow down the accumulation of wrinkles caused by squinting into the sun, as well as provide some protection for your eyes. From about the middle of

May until the first of October, you can usually part with the panty hose and the tie. Most employers will judge your intelligence by your ability to adapt to the environment rather than your ability to sweat. Look for clothes with natural fibers. Cotton, silk, and linen are often the clothes of choice for this reason. It is especially hazardous to leave children or animals inside a car. Temperatures reach dangerous levels in minutes. Leaving the windows open is not adequate. Always take your child with you and when the mercury begins to climb leave your pets elsewhere. When you come in from an outing with the kids, make sure you take a head count to be sure everyone is accounted for. A small child forgotten for even a short time in a hot car doesn't have much of a chance against the heat. Take special care in the summer before buckling children in seat belts, allowing them to climb on metal playground equipment, or walk barefoot on concrete. All of these can be hot enough to burn.

The hottest part of the day usually occurs around 3-4 p.m. You can avoid a lot of heat, by getting things done before noon (or even better before 10 a.m.), otherwise wait until after about six or seven in the evening to venture back outdoors. If there are any delays between your departure from the grocery store and the time you'll be getting home, a cooler in the trunk of your car can give perishables a little extra time to make it home fresh. You can often have a bit of crushed ice packed with your fresh fish selection, just by asking when you make your purchase.

The best time for outdoor summer exercise is between five and seven in the morning. Even your dog knows without anyone telling him, it's cooler in the shade. If you have a couple of blocks to walk and you have the choice of the sunny or the shady side of the street, take the shade. If you're down at the corner waiting for a walk signal, you can usually take a few steps back and into the shade of a building or under an awning. You'll have to arrive early, but shady parking spaces are worth a few extra steps.

If part of your commute to work includes driving east while the sun is on the rise or driving west when the sun is setting, keep your car windshield as clean as possible, this will improve your visibility. Glare is worse if you are looking through a dirty windshield. Keep your sunglasses handy, too.

When you are parking the car, you can keep your car a lot cooler by leaving a window on each side of the car cracked just a fraction of an inch. The inside temperature of the car will stay close to the outside air temperature rather than becoming a heat island. Your insurance agent would probably prefer that you not do this, so be sure you're taking other precautions to deter a theft and don't make it obvious that the windows are open. Sunshades for the car's windshield help hold down the inside temperature and prevent the steering wheel and seat belts from being too hot to touch. There are several types including fold-up cardboard, metallic rollups and spring-loaded fabrics. If you can master the figure-8 fold for the spring-loaded version, it is usually the easiest to use and store. Don't risk burning a small child with a hot car seat. Be sure to check how hot it is before putting your child in. You can lower the temperature quickly with a spray bottle of water. When you first start your car, turn on the air conditioner and open the windows for the first few minutes to blow out the built-up heat. When the car's inside temperature matches the outside air you can raise the windows. If you have leather or vinyl seats, you may want to invest in sheepskin covers for the summer months. Sheepskin will keep you from sticking to the seats and the natural fibers wick away moisture. Even if you are only going across town, toss in a bottle of water. It can be a lifesaver if you or your car overheats or you're stuck waiting for the motor club to come change a tire. Maintaining your car can prevent a lot of problems. You can minimize your risk of a summer breakdown by following these tips. Replace fan belts and radiator hoses every 2 years. Rubber dries out in the heat and low humidity of the desert and can cause cracks. Check for bulges and cracks at regular intervals. Be sure your car has adequate anti-freeze, which not only keeps cooling systems from freezing, but dissipates the heat more efficiently. Change the oil more frequently (every 3,000 miles). Keep the battery clean and filled. Batteries last only about 3 years due to the drying effect of the heat. Replace it as soon as there is any indication that it is about to go. In the heat, car batteries often die without much warning. Car batteries seldom make it to the end of the warranty period in Arizona. Many people replace a battery with one that has a long warranty, knowing that the next battery will be partially paid for.

Window tinting can cut out as much as 50 percent of the heat and ultraviolet rays. If your windows aren't already tinted, metallic film can be installed. Unless you really know what you are doing, have a professional installation. Cracking, peeling window film is a mess. Custom mats for the dash and rear deck can prevent exposed areas from drying out and cracking. A good wax job will protect the car's finish by preventing paint oxidation. If your car doesn't have air conditioning, you might want to trade it for one that does before you move to the low desert. Air conditioning is considered a necessity, not an option, and the resale market for a car without air is not good. You may have the same problem with a black or other dark-colored car. There are more light colored cars in Arizona for a good reason—they stay cooler. Consider a light-colored interior as well. Dark interiors can really hold the heat.

Neither ruthless nor protective, the desert is a neutral environment, where those who dwell within or visit must adapt their behavior to the naturally occurring conditions. The greatest desert dangers are fear, ignorance, and lack of preparation.

Before venturing out in your car, you can reduce your chances of trouble by making sure your car is in good shape. Check tires, belts, and carry hoses. Be sure the radiator has coolant. To ensure your safety, equip your car with items that will be needed if you should become stranded. Bring a minimum of one gallon of water per person per day. Water is more important to your survival than anything else. But it is not enough to carry water–you also need to drink it. Thirst is your body's way of warning you that you are losing water faster than you are replacing it. Desert dwellers learn to heed the warning and respond promptly. Other helpful items include extra oil and water for the car, a tire jack, a tow chain, old carpeting with strong backing, and a small box of non-perishable food.

Leave information about your destination and plans to return with friends or relatives. If you become stranded, remain calm, and rely on your common sense. Rescuers recommend that you stay near your car since a vehicle is easier to spot than a person. If necessary, you can use items from the car to help search crews find you. Mirrors can be used to signal; trunk tools can be used to dig. Aluminum foil also makes a good signaling device. Carpet can be placed under a wheel that is stuck in sand.

Desert survival is a matter of keeping yourself alive. Search and rescue teams rely heavily on the Civil Air Patrol for assistance. If you are lost, you can assist their efforts by burning the spare tire from your trunk to signal for help. Be sure to carry matches in your vehicle. Build a bright evening fire or a smoky daytime fire. Engine oil added to a fire will create heavy smoke, but be extremely careful with fire in the desert for your own safety and to prevent wild fires.

Many organizations offer desert survival classes free or for a minimal charge. If you are unable to attend a class, you can obtain a book on the subject and read it before departing.

DESERT PET PROTECTION

You'll need to protect the family pet from the same risks heat and sun cause for people. Your pet's feet can become blistered from the hot cement or from standing on hot surfaces. Some short-haired dogs may even sunburn. Avoid walking your pet in the heat of the day. Keep a ready supply of water available. Outdoor pets need a supply of fresh water that is always available and an area that is sheltered from the sun. Garage temperatures can reach 140 degrees, so don't count on this as a protective environment. If your pet becomes overheated, he will stop panting, become lethargic and refuse food. These signs call for prompt attention. Get the animal out of the sun. Cover him with a towel soaked in cool water and get him to the vet. Be watchful of older dogs and young puppies around pools. Vision problems may cause an older dog to fall into the pool and drown. Puppies lack the strength and stamina to swim across the pool. If you are going to allow your dog in the backyard pool, take the time to teach him how to find the pool steps to get out on his own. Don't allow access when you are not out to keep an eye on what's happening.

MONSOONS AND FLASH FLOODS

The hot, dry weather of May and June ushers in the "monsoon" season. When warm moist air flows up from the Gulf of Mexico and is heated by Arizona's strong summer sun, thunderstorms occur.

Meteorologists use the dew point to define monsoon days. When the average daily dew point is 55 degrees or higher, the day gets tallied as part of the monsoon season. Generally, July through August marks the monsoon season. The storms typically come in the evening or night and can create havoc in areas where there are no storm sewers. Sometimes the storms are rainless displays of lightning. Heavy, even though brief, rainfall can be followed by flash floods. You are particularly vulnerable in hilly or low terrain. To avoid trouble, stay away from natural streambeds, and other drainage channels during and after rainstorms. Water runs off the higher elevations very rapidly. Never camp on low ground. Know where high ground is and how to get there. Stay out of flooded areas. The National Weather Service has two official warnings regarding flooding:

Flash Flood Watch: Heavy rains may result in flash flooding in the specified area. Be alert and prepared for the possibility of a flood emergency, which will require immediate action.

Flash Flood Warning: Flash flooding is occurring or is imminent in the specified areas. Move to safe ground immediately.

Believe any signs or warnings about flash flood areas!

DUST STORMS

Summer winds sometimes pick up dry, loose dirt particles, creating a dust storm. The reddish-brown clouds vary in density, but can limit drivers' vision.

If dense blowing dust is observed across a roadway, do not enter the area. If you are caught by a dust storm while driving, reduce the speed of your vehicle and carefully pull off the pavement as far as possible. Avoid stopping on the pavement since this is how most chain reaction accidents happen. Turn off your lights and wait until the dust storm has passed. These dust storms are normally followed by rain, which is a signal that you can resume driving.

WINTER STORMS

Between November and April, winter storms are common in Arizona's higher elevations. If you're in areas where snow is possible, be sure you are carrying emergency equipment. The Arizona Department of Transportation recommends that you equip your car with:

- Blankets
- First aid kit
- Containers of water
- Flares
- Flashlight
- Mirror
- Fire extinguisher
- Sunglasses
- Food
- Motor oil
- Maps
- Gloves
- Can opener
- Chains
- Rope
- Electrical tape
- Jumper cables
- Jack, lug wrench
- Spare tire

Other things which may be helpful include:

- Large, empty coffee can with plastic cover (for melting snow)
- Shovel, axe, and knife
- Extra clothing
- Sack of sand or kitty litter
- Two tow chains
- Catalytic heater
- Compass
- Windshield scraper
- Matches and candles
- Small tool kit

SPIDERS, SCORPIONS, LIZARDS, AND SNAKES

Most of the "bugs" you'll meet in Arizona are harmless, and actually serve important roles in keeping nature in balance. Arizona's hot, dry, climate frees residents of many of the bug problems you find in humid areas. You'll also find few rodent problems here. There are a few natives, however, that should be approached cautiously and medical help should be sought immediately if you are bitten.

Black Widows

Shaped like a globe, this spider is black and shiny with red or orange hourglass-shaped markings on its stomach. Its distinctive, strong, irregular-shaped web makes it easy to identify.

Brown Spiders

Often found hiding in closets, under firewood, and under the sink, this spider is about the size of a nickel or a quarter. It has a violin-shaped mark on the back of its head and chest region and is light tan or brown.

Scorpions

Only one of the 15 varieties of scorpions found in Arizona is very dangerous. It is about one and a half inches long and has nearly transparent skin with slender pincers, and a slender tail. While about 1,000 scorpion bites are reported each year, deaths from scorpion bites are almost unheard of.

Lizards

Common and for the most part harmless little creatures, lizards love to sunbathe and climb block walls. The only poisonous species is the Gila monster. It is easily recognizable by its size. About a foot long with a heavy tail and beadlike skin, it is black with shades of orange and pink. If bitten, plunge the area into water to get the Gila monster to loosen its grip, then seek medical attention.

Snakes

There are a number of poisonous snakes in the desert, but very few deaths occur from snakebites. Most cases are the result of the victim attempting to handle or catch the snake.

Rattlesnakes have a large triangular head and usually have a number of rattles on their tail. If you plan to be outdoors frequently, consult a recent first aid manual to be sure you are up-to-date on the latest techniques for treating bites. Most experts recommend getting to a hospital as quickly as possible. Ice packs, tourniquets, sucking out the venom or drinking alcohol are not recommended.

Bites occur more often in April and May when many hibernating creatures emerge to enjoy the spring weather. By summer the animals have reverted to their nocturnal habits and are less likely to be snacking on humans.

The Poison Control Center in Phoenix can be reached at (602) 253-3334 and in Tucson at (520) 626-6016.

POOL SAFETY

Infants and toddlers have a natural attraction to water. It is essential that they have constant supervision when they are near water, and that they do not have access to the water when adults are not close by. Child drowning and near-drowning are alarmingly high in Arizona. To avoid tragedy, follow these precautions:

- Never leave a child alone or near a pool for even a second. In the time it takes to answer the telephone, a child can fall into the pool and drown.
- A fence should bar access to the pool. The fence should be at least four feet high, of material that little feet can't climb, with a self-closing, self-locking latch that young children can't reach. Check your local ordinances. There may be laws that specify fencing requirements.
- Keep toys, particularly tricycles or wheel tools away from the pool. A child playing with these could accidentally fall into the pool.
- Teach your child pool safety habits: No running, pushing, jumping on others, or diving in shallow water. Teach your child and pets the most effective way to get out of the pool quickly.
- Be sure poolside rescue equipment including a flotation ring on a rope or a long handled hook are available to assist in removing a victim from the water. Do not use this equipment for play.
- Do not rely on plastic innertubes, inflatable armbands or other water float toys to prevent accidents.
- Learn Cardiopulmonary Resuscitation (CPR). Infants and toddlers who have taken swimming lessons are not "drown-proof."
- Do not use glass or other breakable containers near the pool.

Chapter 10

NATURE, HISTORY AND ADVENTURE

Variety and abundance characterize Arizona recreation. Even a desert walk may be exciting. More than 1,200 species of wildlife are found in Arizona including elk, bighorn sheep, buffalo, eagles, deer, antelope, mountain lion, bear, turkey, javelina, beaver, geese, and raptors. Bird watchers tally more than 400 feathered species.

State parks as well as national monuments, historic sites, parks, memorials, recreational areas, forests and Indian reservations provide hundreds of entertaining ways to spend a day.

NATIONAL PARKS

Petrified Forest National Park

Location: 25 miles east of Holbrook on I-40

This 160 million-year-old forest contains the largest find of petrified wood in the world. You'll also see the Painted Desert—a rainbow of naturally colored landforms that change with the day's light. It is illegal to remove even the tiniest sliver of petrified wood or any other fossil, archaeological relic, or living plant. A 28-mile road winds through the park. The Rainbow Forest Museum at the south entrance has exhibits of early reptiles, dinosaurs, petrified wood, and a bookstore. Plan to spend two hours at this park.

For more information: (520) 524-6228

The South Rim of the Grand Canyon.

The Grand Canyon

Location: South Rim—At Williams, take AZ 64 north 58 miles
North Rim—45 miles south of Jacob Lake on AZ 67
This is nature at her most impressive. The Colorado River has whittled rock patterns thousands of feet deep, building color kaleidoscopes. The South Rim is open year-round. The North Rim has cooler temperatures, more rainfall, trees, and wildflowers. The park includes 277 miles of the Colorado River and the adjacent uplands. Free shuttle service is available throughout Grand Canyon Village along the West Rim Drive and out to the South Kaibab Trailhead during the peak season (between Memorial and Labor Days).

You can ride the rapids, hike the trails, saddle up on a mule, or helicopter across. There are campgrounds and lodges, including Phantom Ranch at the bottom of the canyon. Visitors are encouraged to make advance reservations. In the busy summer months, facilities are booked far in advance.

For more information: (520) 638-7888

Saguaro National Park

Location: Saguaro East: From I-10 take Broadway or Speedway east to Freeman Rd., turn right on Old Spanish Trail, then left to park entrance (16 miles east of Tucson) Saguaro West: From I-10, take Speedway west (later becomes Gates Pass Rd.). At Kinney Rd., turn right to the park entrance Over 83,000 acres of the world's most majestic plant, the giant saguaro cactus are preserved in areas on either side of Tucson. Both areas put on a spectacular show in May and June when the massive forest is in bloom. Both the East and West units have visitor centers that have slide shows, museum exhibits, cactus gardens and a gift shop. Hiking trails, scenic drives and backcountry camping are featured at each location. Summers are hot, so most visitors come during cooler months.
For more information: (520) 733-5153-east, (520) 733-5158-west

NATIONAL MONUMENTS

Canyon de Chelly National Monument

Location: Just east of Chinle from AZ 191 in northcentral Arizona. This 26-mile stretch of rare beauty is located in the heart of the Navajo reservation. Sandstone walls rise a thousand feet from the canyon floor. Within the canyons, centuries-old Indian ruins (350-1300 A.D.) are preserved. Navajo families still summer on the canyon floor. Opportunities for auto tours, hiking, pictograph viewing, interpretive exhibits and talks, horseback riding, picnicking and photography await visitors. Navajo families still live in the canyon during the summer and can sometimes be spotted with their grazing sheep. Except for the White House Ruins Trail, you'll need a Navajo guide. If accompanied by a guide you can ride through the bottom of the canyon in a four-wheel drive vehicle.
For more information: (520) 674-5500

Casa Grande Ruins National Monument

Location: 1 mile north of Coolidge off AZ 87

Hohokam Indian farmers in the Gila Valley built this four-story building and apartment house 600 years ago. This is one of the largest and most mysterious prehistoric structures ever built in North America. It was also the nation's first archaeological preserve. Evidence of their irrigation canals and the ancient village can still be seen. Temperatures are quite warm in the summer. Allow about an hour to see the monument.

For more information: (520) 723-3172

Chiricahua National Monument

Location: 36 miles southeast of Willcox off AZ 181

Varied rock formations were created millions of years ago by volcanic activity. The Chiricahua Mountains rise steeply from the desert like a forest island. Trails provide views of all the park's features. There is a visitor's center, campgrounds, scenic drives, hiking trails, self-guided trails, and picnic areas are available. Hikers and birdwatchers find this biologically diverse area a paradise. The Chihuahuan and Sonoran deserts meet here, as do the Rocky Mountains and Mexico's northern Sierra Madre. Javelina, coatamundi, hog-nosed and hooded skunks, white-tailed deer, bears and mountain lions make this area their home. Hummingbirds, orioles, tanager, redstarts, warblers, and grosbeaks are among the bird population. Faraway Ranch gives a glimpse of pioneer life. The house is furnished with historic artifacts.

For more information: (520) 824-3560

Montezuma's Castle National Monument

Location: 5 miles northeast of Camp Verde, take Exit 289 from I-17

A five-story 19-room cliff dwelling remains ninety percent intact.

Early settler's mistakenly associated the structure with the Aztec emperor Montezuma, but study indicates the prehistoric Sinaguan "high rise apartment" building was in place almost a century earlier. About a million visitors come each year, most in the spring. Allow about an hour to visit. A second part of the Monument, Montezuma's Well, is located 7 miles to the north. Visitors to the well see a large natural limestone sink with a deep pool of water in what is an otherwise dry plateau.

For more information: (520) 567-3322

Navajo National Monument

Location: 9 miles north of Black Mesa Junction on AZ 564
Located on the Navajo Indian Reservation in northeastern Arizona, the monument contains some of the best Anasazi ruins on the Colorado Plateau. Betatakin and Keet Seel are open when weather permits. Inscription House is closed due to its fragile condition. The spectacular cliff dwellings date from seven centuries ago. While the monument is open year round, winter snowfall is about 60 inches and may not be the best time to come. Only 20 permits are issued for the 17-mile Keet Seel hike and 25 for the strenuous 5-mile hike to Betatakin each day. Betatakin can also be viewed from an overlook requiring only a 1-mile walk.

For more information: (520) 672-2366

Organ Pipe Cactus National Monument

Location: 22 miles south of Why
The monument is named for the cactus species found here that resembles the pipes of an organ. This is a Biosphere Reserve offering a pristine example of the Sonoran Desert. There are six varieties of rattlesnakes as well as Gila monsters and scorpions living here, so keep your eyes on your surroundings. The 21-mile

Ajo Mountain Drive and the 53-mile Puerto Blanco Drive wind up and down graded dirt roads allowing visitors to take in the harsh yet beautiful desert land that is home to cactus and desert wildlife. If you choose the Puerto Blanco Drive you will find the desert oasis of Quitobaquito which offers exceptional bird watching. On the third Saturday in March the Tohono O'Odham Celebration takes place. Native Americans demonstrate traditional arts and crafts such as basket making, pottery, dryland farming, dancing, and story telling.
For more information: (520) 387-6849

Pipe Spring National Monument
Location: In the Arizona Strip 14 miles southwest of Fredonia off AZ 389
A desert oasis, with four springs located nearby, water has drawn people to this area for centuries. First came the Pueblo and Paiute Indians, and later an historic Mormon fort was located at this site. The well-preserved fort and other structures were built in the early 1870s. This is a living history ranch. Most visitors come in the summer including many birds who are lured to the area by the springs.
For more information: (520) 643-7105

Sunset Crater National Monument
Location: 14 miles northeast Flagstaff just off US 89
This volcanic cinder cone rises 1,000 feet above the surface. Made from colorful red and orange cinders and formed before 1100 AD. Because of the fragile nature of the volcano, hiking and climbing are prohibited. Other cinder cones in the area are accessible. It is often windy here and temperature changes can occur rapidly. Lava Flow Trail is a self-guided loop just a third of a mile long. Lenox Crater Trail provides an opportunity to climb on a cinder cone. Be careful when hiking on lava. It is sharp, brittle, and unstable.
For more information: (520) 526-0502

Tonto National Monument

Location: 28 miles northwest of Globe just off AZ 88

Well-preserved cliff dwellings occupied by the Salado Indians during the 13th, 14th and early 15th century overlook Roosevelt Lake. The Salado Indians farmed, hunted, and gathered native wildlife and plants. They were craftsmen noted for polychrome pottery and intricately woven textiles, many of which are on display in the monument museum. Located in the Upper Sonoran ecosystem, saguaro cactus are a prominent landscape feature. You'll also see cholla, prickly pear, hedgehog, and barrel cactus. Spring wildflowers can be spectacular here.

For more information: (520) 467-2241

Tuzigoot National Monument

Location: From I-17, take Exit 287 west on AZ 260 to Cottonwood, take Main St. north towards Clarkdale

Tuzigoot is an ancient village built by the Sinagua Indians. The pueblo has 110 rooms, including second and third story structures. The earliest rooms were built around 1000 A.D. The Sinagua were a farming and trading community. They left the colorful Verde Valley around 1400 AD. Adjacent to Tuzigoot is Tavasci Marsh, a critically important habitat for birds and wildlife including beaver, river otter, muskrat, deer, javelina, fish, amphibians and birds.

For more information: (520) 634-5564

Walnut Canyon National Monument

Location: From Flagstaff take I-40, At Exit 204 go 7.5 miles east, then 3 miles south

Built into the canyon's limestone walls over 300 cliff dwellings show the masonry skills of the Sinagua Indians. Visitors experience the serenity and scenic beauty found here 800 years ago.

For more information: (520) 526-3367

Wupatki National Monument

Location: From Flagstaff, take US 89 north 12 miles, turn right at Sunset Crater Volcano/Wupatki National Monument. The Visitor Center is 14 miles from here.

Ancient Indian farmers lived and tilled the soil in the area around the San Francisco Peaks. The Sinagua and Anasazi Indians lived in this region until 1200 A.D. About 2,000 archaeological sites are scattered within the monument. Sunsets are spectacular here.

For more information: (520) 679-2365

NATIONAL HISTORIC PARKS

Tumacacori National Historic Park

Location: 3 miles south of Tubac, take Exit 29 from I-19

Originally a mission founded in 1697 by Father Eusebio Kino. The site was later administered by the Franciscans. Exhibits at the monument show how Spanish culture was introduced to southern Arizona's indigenous people. Today visitors see the massive adobe ruin built in the early 1800s. You'll also see dioramas, santos and objects related to the Kino missions in the area. During the winter months guided tours are available. Local and Mexican artisans demonstrate traditional crafts. On the first weekend in December the Fiesta at Tumacacori is held. In April and October a traditional High Mass is held. Advance reservations are required for the Masses.

For more information: (520) 398-2341

NATIONAL HISTORIC SITES

Fort Bowie National Historic Site

Location: 12 miles south of Bowie on I-10

Fort Bowie includes a cluster of adobe buildings that were constructed in 1862 to secure the Apache Pass. This area was the heart of military operations against Geronimo and his band of Apaches. The site is accessible from a rugged 1.5 mile hiking trail.

For more information: (520) 847-2500

Hubbell Trading Post National Historic Site
Location: 1 mile west of Ganado
John Lorenzo Hubbell began trading with the Navajo Indians in 1876 shortly after their internment at Fort Sumner. Hubbell gained the Indians respect and often acted in their behalf. The Hubbell family operated the post until it was sold to the National Park Service in 1967. Today the trading post serves Native American residents as well as tourists. You'll find an excellent display of Navajo crafts and hear the melodic Navajo language in use.

For more information: (520) 755-3475

NATIONAL MEMORIALS

Coronado National Memorial
Location: Near the Mexican border just west of AZ 92
This memorial recognizes Francisco Vasquez Coronado's first major European expedition into the American Southwest. The memorial lies on the U.S.-Mexico border within sight of the San Pedro River Valley. Expansive views of the region are in store for visitors. There is a small museum with authentic and replica 16th Century arms and armor.

For more information: (520) 366-5515

NATIONAL RECREATION AREAS

Glen Canyon National Recreation Area
Location: Area surrounding Lake Powell

Lake Powell is the second largest man-made lake in the United States. Glen Canyon was flooded with waters from the Colorado River to form the lake. Houseboats, sailboats, and motorboats share the water. The recreation area stretches hundreds of miles from Lees Ferry in Arizona to the Orange Cliffs of southern Utah. From the beginning the Glen Canyon Dam has been a controversial environmental issue and is still debated today. It gets hot here in the summer with very little shade. The visitor centers feature exhibits on construction of the dam, history of the area during the Ice Age, and the dinosaurs who once roamed the area. You'll also find information on geology, slot canyons, Native Americans and pioneers.

For more information: (520) 608-6404

Lake Mead National Recreation Area
Location: Area surrounding Lake Mead and Lake Mohave

Lake Mead is the largest artificial lake in the United States. Water sports, hiking, camping are on tap here. The three of the four major desert ecosystems found in the United States meet here: the Mohave, the Great Basin and the Sonoran Desert. Bighorn sheep, mule deer, coyotes, kit foxes, bobcats, ringtail cats, desert tortoise, and peregrine falcon are found here.

For more information: (702) 293-8920

NATIONAL FORESTS

Apache Sitgreaves National Forest

Location: Central/Eastern Arizona

This two million acre forest encompasses magnificent mountain country in east-central Arizona along the Mogollon Rim and the White Mountains. The forest has 24 lakes and reservoirs and more than 450 miles of rivers and streams. The General Crook Trail, the main supply route for U.S. Army forts in New Mexico and Arizona runs through the forest. Mount Baldy, Escudilla, and Bear Wallow Wildernesses and the Blue Range Primitive Area make this one of the country's premier backcountry forests.

For more information: P.O. Box 640, Springerville, AZ 85938, (520) 333-4301

Coconino National Forest

Location: Near Flagstaff

The Coconino Forest offers 1.8 million acres for hiking, backpacking, trail riding (horses and bikes), camping, picnicking, boating and fishing. In the winter snowshoes go on and the cross-country and alpine skis come out. There are many distinct environments including the volcanic highlands with high country mountain forests and meadows (which reach 12,643 at the top of the San Francisco Peaks); the plateau country with wide open spaces dotted by lakes; the Mogollon Rim with lush forest on the edge of a long steep cliff; the desert canyon country, with deep wilderness gorges; and red rock country near Sedona.

For more information: (520) 527-3500

Coronado National Forest

Location: Scattered areas in southern Arizona

More than 1.7 million acres of Southern Arizona and New Mexico are included in the Coronado National Forest. You can be in hot, arid desert and in less than an hour have reached the cool pines. There are rolling grasslands and conifer forests. Elevations range from 2,400 to 10,500 feet. Twelve mountain ranges can be found within this forest. These mountains are sometimes referred to as "sky islands" because of the way they rise from the desert floor.

For more information: (520) 670-4552

Kaibab National Forest

Location: North/Central Arizona

Bordering both the North and South Rims of the Grand Canyon, the Kaibab Forest covers more than 1.6 million acres. Elevations range from 5,500 to 10,418 feet at Kendrick Peak. The forest is filled with breathtaking views, outstanding forest scenery, and unusual geologic formations. Elk, mule deer, antelope, turkey, coyote are fairly common in the forest. On rare occasions mountain lion, black bear and bobcat are spotted.

For more information: (520) 635-8200

Prescott National Forest

Location: Central/Western Arizona

The Prescott National Forest can be best described as nearly 1.25 million acres of cool relief from the desert just below it. There are year-round opportunities for camping, picnicking, fishing, hunting, scenic drives, photography, mountain climbing, hiking and horseback riding.

For more information: (520) 771-4700

Tonto National Forest

Location: Central/Eastern Arizona.

One of the largest forests in America, the Tonto National Forest covers nearly three million acres of rugged, scenic landscapes ranging from cactus-studded desert to pine-clad mountains. Elevations range from 1,300 to 8,000 feet. This is the country popularized in Zane Grey novels. Six man-made reservoirs on the Salt and Verde Rivers in addition to the rivers that flow into them offer opportunities for boating, sailing, water skiing, swimming, rafting and tubing. World class white water rafting is found along the upper stretches of the Salt River. The Apache Trail Scenic Byway is brimming with history and scenery. Portions of the Verde River have been designated as a Wild and Scenic River. More than 400 wildlife species including eight endangered species make their home here. Hunting and fishing opportunities are abundant, Deer, javelina, and game birds such as Canadian geese and quail are found here. There are trout in the cold mountain lakes and streams, bass in the warm desert lakes. Trails open to horses and hikers are plentiful. Most forest areas are open to camping and there are developed campgrounds. Ranger districts are located in Cave Creek, Globe, Mesa, Payson, Pleasant Valley and along the Tonto Basin. **For more information:** (602)225-5200

STATE PARKS

Thousands of acres of scenic Arizona await visitors to Arizona's state parks. There are nominal admission fees to enter the state's historic, interpretive and recreational parks. Frequent visitors may purchase an annual use day permit. For general information about the state park system write or phone:

Arizona State Parks
1300 W. Washington
Phoenix, AZ 85007
(602) 542-4174

Arizona's State Parks

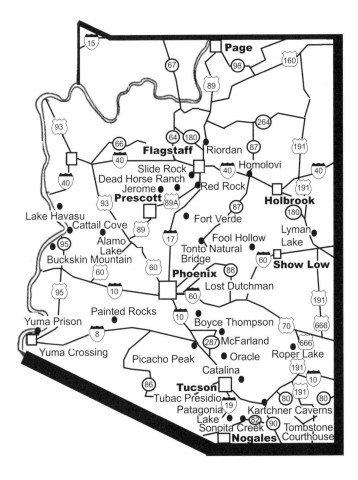

Alamo Lake State Park

Location: 38 miles northwest of Wenden and US 60
Size: 8,400 Acres   **Elevation:** 1,250 Feet
Attractions: Boating, fishing, hiking, camping. Alamo Lake is known for excellent bass, catfish and bluegill fishing. This desert lake is used as a flood control reservoir along the Bill Williams River, just 30 miles before it joins the Colorado River. Water levels do fluctuate here. The Rawhide and Buckskin Mountains are nearby. Wildlife in the area include quail, deer, coyote, bald eagles and wild burros. There is a marina store with boat rentals.
For more information: (520) 669-2088

Boyce Thompson Arboretum

Location: 3 miles west of Superior on US 60
Size: 420 acres   **Elevation:** 2,400 Feet
Attractions: Botanic garden, museum, hiking, and nature trails, picnic area. This Arboretum is a desert museum displaying hundreds of plant varieties from arid lands throughout the world. The arboretum is a major research center for arid plant research. Walking trails pass alongside interesting plant forms. Visitors can purchase cactus and succulents at the garden's visitor center.
For more information: (520) 689-2723

Buckskin Mountain State Park

Location: 11 miles north of Parker on AZ 95
Size: 1,676 Acres   **Elevation:** 420 Feet
Attractions: Boating, fishing, swimming, water skiing, hiking, nature trails, and camping. Buckskin Mountain State Park is set among scenic bluffs overlooking the Colorado River. Desert bighorn sheep make their home in the Buckskin Mountain range. Coyotes, jackrabbits and even rattlesnakes are in abundance at this park.
For more information: (520) 667-3231

Catalina State Park

Location: Just north of Tucson on US 89
Size: 5,511 Acres   **Elevation:** 2,650 Feet
Attractions: Camping, picnicking, and bird watching. Hiking, nature and horse trails in Catalina State Park are near the base of the northwestern slopes of the Catalina Mountains near Tucson. Horses can be loaded and unloaded in the park's parking and staging area. There is trail access to the Coronado National Forest. These foothills, canyons and streams are the home of more than 150 species of birds.
For more information: (520) 628-5798

Cattail Cove State Park

Location: 15 miles south of Lake Havasu City, from AZ 95
Size: 5,500 Acres   **Elevation:** 450 Feet
Attractions: 40-site campground, 150 boat camps.
Getting away from it all takes on new meaning when campers must find their sites by boat. Huge shade trees and versatile topography attract visitors.
For more information: (520) 855-1223

Dead Horse Ranch State Park

Location: Across the river from Cottonwood, enter from N. Fifth St.
Size: 320 Acres   **Elevation:** 3,300 Feet
Attractions: Historic site, museum, fishing, hiking, nature trails, and camping. Visitors to Dead Horse Ranch State Park have a choice of stream and pond fishing, bird watching or trails for hiking in the midst of shady cottonwood groves along the Verde River.
For more information: (520) 634-5283

Fool Hollow Lake Recreation Area

Location: Near Show Low
Size: 800 acres   **Elevation:** 6,300 feet
Attractions: Camping, hiking, fishing, picnic areas.
For more information: (520) 537-3680

Fort Verde State Historic Park

Location: In Camp Verde, 3 miles east of I-17
Size: 11 Acres   **Elevation:** 3,150 Feet
Attractions: Historic site and museum. During the Indian campaigns of the 1870s Fort Verde was headquarters for General George Crook's scouts, soldiers and pack mules.
For more information: (520) 567-3275

Homolovi Ruins State Park

Location: 5 miles northeast of Winslow off AZ 87
Size: 4,500 Acres   **Elevation:** 4,900 Feet
Attractions: Camping, picnicking, hiking, equestrian trails. This is Arizona's first state archaeological park. The word Homolovi is Hopi for "place of the mounds." The park has four major pueblo sites thought to have been occupied by the Hopi between 200 and 1425 A.D. There are more than 340 sites within the park. Ongoing archaeological research takes place here.
For more information: (520) 289-4106

Jerome State Historic Park

Location: In Jerome, off AZ 89A
Size: 3 Acres   **Elevation:** 5,000 Feet
Attractions: Historic site and museum. The Jerome State Park is located at the mansion once owned by James S. "Rawhide" Douglas. Panoramic views of Jerome and Verde Valley and exhibits recounting the copper mining community's history for visitors.
For more information: (520) 634-5381

Kartchner Caverns State Park

Location: 8 miles south of I-10 off AZ 90 near Benson
Size: 550 acres   **Elevation:** 4,000 Feet
A spectacular limestone cave more than 2 miles long draped in reds, browns and oranges. The cave features numerous long, thin extremely fragile formations, known as "soda straws" and 10-12 foot stalagmite and stalactites. Under development since 1988, the park was scheduled to open in November, 1999.
For more information: (602) 542-4174

Lake Havasu State Park Windsor Beach

Location: At Lake Havasu, across from London Bridge
Size: 6,300 Acres   **Elevation:** 450 Feet
Attractions: Boating, fishing, hiking, nature trails, and marina group campgrounds are available here.
For more information: (520) 855-2784

Lost Dutchman State Park

Location: 6 miles northeast of Apache Junction on AZ 88
Size: 292 Acres   **Elevation:** 2,000 Feet
Attractions: Hiking, nature trails, and camping. Lost Dutchman State Park lies at the base of the Superstition Mountains. Tales of searching for the Lost Dutchman's Gold Mine abound in the area.
For more information: (602) 982-4485

Lyman Lake State Park

Location: 11 miles south of St. Johns, 1 mile from US 191
Size: 1,180 Acres   **Elevation:** 6,000 Feet
Attractions: Boating, fishing, hiking, nature trails, swimming beach, and camping. Fishing enthusiasts will find walleye, northern pike, largemouth bass, channel catfish and crappie at Lyman Lake State Park. A small herd of buffalo are often spotted near the access road.
For more information: (520) 337-4441

McFarland State Historic Park

Location: In Florence, off US 89 and AZ 287
Size: 2 Acres   **Elevation:** 1,500 Feet
Attractions: Historic site.
Located in the old town of Florence, this park features the original adobe Pinal County Courthouse built in 1878. Collections of Arizona pioneering lawyer and politician Ernest W. McFarland are housed here.
For more information: (520) 868-5216

Oracle State Park

Location: 1 mile east of Oracle off Mt. Lemmon Rd.
Size: 4,000 Acres   **Elevation:** 4,200 Feet
Still under development this land was once held by the Defenders of Wildlife. Oracle State Park is used as an environmental education center and a wildlife refuge. The park is not currently open to visitors unless they are involved in the education programs. The park consists of oak grassland, riparian woodland and mesquite scrub habitats with diverse wildlife and plants.
For more information: (520) 896-2425

Patagonia Lake State Park

Location: 12 miles east of Nogales on AZ 82, 4 miles north on gravel road
Size: 640 Acres   **Elevation:** 4,000 Feet
Attractions: Boating, swimming, fishing, water skiing, hiking, nature trails, camping, and marina. Located in the beautiful Sonoita Valley, Patagonia State Park is one of the most attractive recreational areas in the state.
For more information: (520) 287-6965

Picacho Peak State Park

Location: 40 miles north of Tucson along I-10

Size: 3,400 Acres   **Elevation:** 2,000 Feet

Attractions: Historic site, hiking, nature trails, and camping. Picacho Peak's sharp-sided 1500-foot peak can be seen rising from the desert floor for miles. It has been a landmark for Arizona travelers for many years, and is known for colorful spring wildflowers. Picacho Peak was the site of the only Civil War battle fought in Arizona.

For more information: (520) 466-3183

Red Rock State Park

Location: South of Sedona off Red Rock Loop Rd.

Size: 286 Acres   **Elevation:** 3,900 Feet

Attractions: Hiking, picnicking, environmental study center Red Rock State Park is nestled along Oak Creek among green meadows and red cliffs. Hikers, picnickers and photographers will enjoy this site.

For more information: (520) 282-6907

Cathedral Rock from Red Rock Loop Road Crossing.

Riordan State Historic Park

Location: In Flagstaff on Riordan Ranch St.
Size: 5 Acres   **Elevation:** 6,900 Feet
Attractions: Historic homes. This historic park include the homes of prominent northern Arizona residents Michael and Timothy Riordan which were linked by a "rendezvous wing." The homes provide a glimpse at rustic elegance enjoyed in the early 1900s. The home is a good example of Craftsman style architecture.
For more information: (520) 779-4395

Roper Lake State Park

Location: 4 miles south of Safford, one half mile east of US 191
Size: 319 Acres   **Elevation:** 3,130 Feet
Attractions: Boating, swimming, fishing, hiking, nature trails, and camping. The man-made lake at Roper Lake State Park is brimming with bass, bluegill and catfish. Boaters are welcome, but are limited to oars, sails or electric motors. Located at the foot of Mount Graham, one of Arizona's highest peaks, you'll find natural hot springs at the lake's edge.
For more information: (520) 428-6760

Slide Rock State Park

Location: 7 miles north of Sedona on Highway 89A
Size: 43 Acres   **Elevation:** 4,930 Feet
Attractions: Natural waterslide, picnicking, fishing and photography. Set among red rock mountains, pine trees, green meadows and a large orchard, visitors relax and enjoy nature at its most magnificent. The park provides habitats for more than 100 species of birds. This is a very popular summer stop, try to come during the week to avoid some of the crowds. The slide area is very slippery and missteps can easily happen. So hold onto children or they'll be floating downstream without you.
For more information: (520) 282-3034

Sonoita Creek Natural Area

Location: Near Patagonia Lake State Park

Size: 5,000 Acres   **Elevation:** 4,000 Feet

Attractions: Considered a significant riparian area, with giant cottonwoods, willows, sycamores and mesquites, this area is still under development and an opening date for the area has not yet been set. It is expected to be used for hiking, wildlife viewing, environmental educational programs and research.

For more information: (602) 542-4174

Tombstone Courthouse State Historic Park

Location: In Tombstone, off US 80

Size: 1 Acre   **Elevation:** 4,539 Feet

Attractions: Historic site and museum. Tombstone Courthouse State Historic Park features a stylish Victorian building, constructed in 1882. The building is filled with exhibits recalling Arizona's turbulent 1880s.

For more information: (520) 457-331

Tonto Natural Bridge State Park

Location: 13 miles northwest of Payson off AZ 87

Size: 160 acres   **Elevation:** 4,800 Feet

Attractions: Natural bridge, historic lodge, picnic facilities and hiking trails. One of the largest travertine bridges, this natural limestone arch soars 183 feet above Pine Creek. Tonto Natural Bridge is a day-use only park. Fern-filled grottoes, and grassy meadows are some of nature's lures to this location. A restored 1900s hotel is located here.

For more information: (520) 476-4202

Tubac Presidio State Historic Park

Location: Near Tubac, off I-19
Size: 10 Acres   **Elevation:** 3,500 Feet
Attractions: Historic site and museum. The Tubac Presidio highlights what remains of an historic military fort established by the Spaniards in 1752. The fort was used in an attempt to control local Pima and Apache Indians as well as for a base in exploring the Southwest.
For more information: (520) 398-2252

Yuma Crossing State Historic Park

Location: In Yuma. From I-8 take the Fourth Ave. exit south. Cross the Colorado River and the park is on the east side of Fourth Ave.
Size: 20 Acres   **Elevation:** 140 Feet
Attractions: Museum, picnic area. The area was the center of the comings and goings along the Colorado River for five centuries. It was first inhabited by the prehistoric Patayan culture followed by the Quechan Native Americans, Spanish explorers, mountain men, gold seekers, soldiers, muleskinners, railroaders, steamboat captains and shippers—all of whom needed to cross the Colorado River.
For more information: (520) 329-0471

Yuma Territorial Prison State Historic Park and Quartermaster Depot

Location: In Yuma, off I-8
Size: 19 Acres   **Elevation:** 141 Feet
Attractions: Historic site and museum. The Yuma Territorial Prison shows vividly how Arizona convicts served time in early Arizona. There are strap-iron and granite cell blocks and cells dug out of rock-hard caliche. The Yuma Quartermaster Depot stored and distributed supplies for all the military posts in Arizona and posts in Nevada, Utah, New Mexico and Texas in the late 1800s.
For more information: (520) 783-4771

INDIAN RESERVATIONS

Most of Arizona's Indian tribes welcome visitors. Keep in mind that visitors are expected to honor the customs and culture of the people whose reservation they are visiting. Please ask permission before taking photographs.

Arizona's Indian Reservations

1. Hopi
2. Navajo
3. San Juan Southern
   Paiute
4. Havasupai
5. Hualapai
6. Kaibab-Paiute
7. Fort Mojave
8. Yavapai Prescott
9. Tonto-Apache
10. Camp Verde
    Yavapai-Apache
11. Colorado River
12. Fort Yuma-Quechan
13. Cocopah
14. Gila Bend
15. Gila River
16. Fort McDowell
17. Salt River
18. Ak-Chin
19. Tohono O'Odham
20. Pascua-Yaqui
21. San Xavier
22. San Carlos
23. White Mountain
    Apache

Ak-Chin Reservation

Location: 56 miles south of Phoenix in Pinal County
Tribe: Papago-Pima
Known for: Basketry
Attractions: Harrah's Al-Chin Casino, Eco-museum, Bekol Commissary, St. Francis Church Feast, October 4, Tribal Election Barbecue, the second Saturday in January
For more information:
> Ak-Chin Indian Community
> 42507 W. Peters and Nall Rd.
> Maricopa, AZ 85239
> (520) 568-2227

Camp Verde Yavapai-Apache Reservation

Location: 95 miles northwest of Phoenix
Tribe: Yavapai
Known for: Basketry
Attractions: Montezuma Castle National Monument, Montezuma Well and Tuzigoot, Cliff Castle Lodge and Casino
For more information:
> Yavapai Apache Tribe
> 3435 Shaw Ave.
> Camp Verde, AZ 86322
> (520) 567-3649

Cocopah Reservation

Location: 13 miles south of Yuma
Tribe: Cocopahs
Known for: Beadwork
Attractions: Heritage Art Museum, Pow Wow, RV park, Cocopah Casino

For more information:
Cocopah Tribal Council
County 15th and Ave. G
Somerton, AZ 85350
(520) 627-2102

Colorado River Reservation

Location: Parker
Tribes: Chemehuevi, Mojave
Known for: Basketry, beadwork, and Indian-motif wall clocks
Attractions: Blue Water Casino, Arts and Crafts Center, 100 miles of river frontage, boat races, water sports, All-Indian Rodeo, Indian Day Celebration, dove and quail hunting, fishing, picnicking, water sports
For more information:
Colorado River Indian Tribes
Rt. 1, Box 23-B
Parker, AZ 85344
(520) 669-9211

Fort McDowell Reservation

Location: 36 miles east of Phoenix in Maricopa County
Tribe: Mojave-Apache
Known for: Basketry
Attractions: Verde River, The Fort Casino, camping, fishing, tubing
For more information:
Mojave-Apache Tribal Council
P.O. Box 17779
Fountain Hills, AZ 85268
(480) 837-5121

Fort Mojave Reservation
Location: 236 miles northwest of Phoenix in Mohave County
Tribe: Mojave
Known for: Basketry and beadwork
Attractions: Avi Hotel and Casino, water sports, dove and quail hunting, picnicking, camping, and water sports, Fort Mojave Indian Days, Pow Wow, nearby sand dunes
For more information:
> Fort Mojave Tribal Council
> 500 Merrimam Ave.
> Needles, CA 92363
> (760) 629-4591

Fort Yuma-Quechan Reservation
Location: near Yuma
Tribe: Yuma
Known for: Beadwork and artifacts
Attractions: Quechan Indian Museum, bingo hall, casino, RV parks, Colorado River, fishing, picnicking, water sports, camping, nearby sand dunes
For more information:
> Fort Yuma Quechan Tribe
> P.O. Box 11352
> Yuma, AZ 85366
> (520) 572-0213

Gila River Reservation
Location: Sacaton, 40 miles south of Phoenix
Tribes: Pima, Maricopa
Known for: Pima basketry and Maricopa pottery
Attractions: Wild Horse Pass and Lone Butte Casinos, Gila River

Arts and Crafts Center, Gila Heritage Village and Museum, Firebird Lake and Water Sports Marina, Mul-Cha-Tha (Gathering of the People), Rodeo and Miss Gila River Pageant, St. John's Mission Fair

For more information:

> Gila River Community
> P.O. Box 97
> Sacaton, AZ 85247
> (520) 562-3311

Havasupai Reservation

Location: 266 miles northwest of Phoenix in Coconino County
Tribe: Havasupai
Known for: Basketry and beadwork
Attractions: Waterfalls, turquoise pools, gorges and canyons. It's an 8-mile trail from Hilltop to Supai by pack horses, on foot, or by helicopter to reach the reservation. The people of the "Blue-Green Waters" are located at the bottom of Havasupai Canyon, a tributary of the Grand Canyon. Advance reservations are required

For more information:

> Havasupai Tribal Council
> P.O. Box 10
> Supai, AZ 86435
> (520) 448-2961

Hopi Reservation

Location: 260 miles northeast of Phoenix in Coconino and Navajo Counties
Tribe: Hopi
Known for: Kachina dolls, basketry, pottery, overlay jewelry, silver crafts, and weaving. The Hopi tribe has lived in Arizona for more than 2,000 years. The village of Old Oraibi is the oldest continually inhabited village in North America.

Attractions: Cultural Center, Ceremonials
For more information:
> Hopi Tribal Council
> P.O. Box 123
> Kykotsmovi, AZ 86039
> (520) 734-2441

Hualapai Reservation
Location: 205 miles northwest of Phoenix in Coconino, Yavapai and Mohave Counties
Tribe: Hualapai
Known for: Basketry, dolls
Attractions: Camping, hiking, hunting, fishing, white water trips on the Colorado River
For more information:
> Hualapai Tribal Council
> P.O. Box 179
> Peach Springs, AZ 86434
> (520) 769-2216

Kaibab-Paiute Reservation
Location: 350 miles north of Phoenix in Mohave County
Tribe: Kaibab-Paiute
Known for: Coiled, shallow baskets known as "Wedding Baskets"
Attractions: Pipe Springs National Monument, Steamboat Rock, RV park and campground
For more information:
> Kaibab-Paiute Tribal Council
> HC 65 Box 2
> Fredonia, AZ 86002
> (520) 643-7245

Navajo Reservation

Location: 260 miles northeast of Phoenix in Apache, Coconino, and Navajo Counties
Tribe: Navajo
Known for: Blanket, tapestry weaving, silver crafts, and basketry
Attractions: Monument Valley, Canyon de Chelly, Little Colorado River Gorge, Grand Falls, Rainbow Bridge, Navajo National Monument, Betatakin, Window Rock, Four Corners, Hubbell Trading Post, Ceremonials, Rodeo & Art Fair, arts and craft shops, camping, hunting, fishing, hiking
For more information:
> Navajoland Tourism Dept.
> P.O. Box 663
> Window Rock, AZ 86515
> (520) 871-6436

Pascua-Yaqui Reservation

Location: 135 miles southwest of Phoenix in Pima County
Tribe: Yaqui
Known for: Deer Dance statues and children's cultural paintings
Attractions: Casino of the Sun, Easter Ceremonial, September Recognition Ceremonial
For more information:
> Pascua-Yaqui Tribal Council
> 7474 S. Camino de Oeste
> Tucson, AZ 85746
> (520) 883-5000

Salt River Reservation
Location: 15 miles northeast of Phoenix in Maricopa County
Tribe: Pima, Maricopa
Known for: Basketry and pottery
Attractions: Hoo-hoogam Ki Museum, the Pavilions Shopping Center, Casino Arizona, rodeo, tubing, camping, picnicking on the Salt River
For more information:
> Salt River-Maricopa Tribal Council
> 10005 E. Osborne Rd.
> Scottsdale, AZ 85256
> (480) 850-8000

San Carlos Reservation
Location: 115 miles northeast of Phoenix in Gila and Graham Counties
Tribe: Apache
Known for: Basketry, beadwork, and peridot jewelry
Attractions: San Carlos Lake—fishing, camping, and hunting, white water rafting, kayaking and canoeing along the Salt River, Cultural Center, Apache Gold Casino, rodeos
For more information:
> San Carlos Apache Tribal Council
> P.O. Box O
> San Carlos, AZ 85550
> (520) 475-2361

San Juan Southern Paiute Reservation
Location: East of the Grand Canyon, between the San Juan and Colorado Rivers (near Tuba City)
Tribe: Paiute
Known for: Hand-woven baskets
Attractions: Native basketweaving, Paiute Canyon, Pow Wow. This tribe of only 250 members is newly recognized and many members live on the Navajo Reservation.
For more information:
    San Juan Southern Paiute Tribe
    P.O. Box 1989
    Tuba City, Arizona 86045
    (520) 283-4587

Tohono O'Odham Reservation
Location: 136 miles south of Phoenix in Maricopa, Pinal, and Pima Counties
Tribe: Tohono O'Odham
Known for: Basketry and pottery
Attractions: Desert Diamond Casino, Kitt Peak National Observatory, Ventana Caves, Topawa Mission, Organ Pipe National Monument, Forteleza Ruins, Mission San Xavier Del Bac, Indian arts and crafts market, Baboquivari rodeo & fair, Papago Village Solar Power Project
For more information:
    Tohono O'Odham Tribal Nation
    P.O. Box 837
    Sells, AZ 85634
    (520) 627-2101

Tonto-Apache Reservation
Location: 94 miles northeast of Phoenix in Gila County near Payson
Tribe: Apache
Known for: Basketry and beadwork
Attractions: Hiking and picnicking, Mazatzal Casino
For more information:
Tonto-Apache Tribal Council
Tonto Apache Reservation #30
Payson, AZ 85541
(520) 474-5000

White Mountain Apache Reservation
Location: 194 miles northeast of Phoenix in Apache, Gila, and Navajo Counties
Tribe: Apache
Known for: Basketry (Burden Baskets) and beadwork
Attractions: Salt River Canyon, Sunrise Ski Resort, Hon-Dah Casino (near Pinetop), Fort Apache and Cultural Museum, Kinishba Ruins, Annual Rodeo and Fair (Labor Day Weekend), ceremonials, rafting, camping, fishing, hunting, skiing, horseback riding, hiking
For more information:
White Mountain Apache Tribe
P.O. Box 710
Fort Apache, AZ 85926
(520) 338-1230

Yavapai Prescott Reservation

Location: 103 miles northwest of Phoenix
Tribe: Yavapai
Known for: Basketry
Attractions: Bucky's Casino, Yavapai Gaming Center, Prescott Resort Conference Center & Casino, hiking and picnicking, Pow Wow
For more information:

Yavapai-Prescott Tribal Council
530 E. Merritt St.
Prescott, AZ 86301
(520) 445-8790

Appendix A

ONE-STOP
CAREER CENTERS

Many new One-Stop Career Centers have been opened recently and others are expected to open. This list may no longer be current. Please check the government section of your local phone book if you need more information. Career Centers may be listed under State Government, Department of Economic Security or under County or City Government. In some counties there are more than one location.

Mohave County Career Center
201 N. 4th St.
Kingman, AZ 86401
(520)753-0723

Coconino Career Center
2625 N. King St.
Flagstaff, AZ 86004
(520)522-7900

Show Low Center
40 S. 11th St.
Show Low, AZ 85901
(520)537-2948

Winslow Center
319 E. Third St.
Winslow, AZ 86047
(520)289-4644

Apache County Work First
1359 E. Main St.
Springerville, AZ 85938
(520)333-5526

Prescott Center
234 Grove Ave.
Prescott, AZ 86301
(520) 445-5100

Cottonwood Center
1645 E Cottonwood Ste.E
Cottonwood, AZ 86326
(520)634-3337

La Paz One-Stop Career Center
1113 Kofa Ave.
Parker, AZ 85344
(520)669-9812

Yuma Career Resource Center
3826 W. 16th St.
Yuma, AZ 85364
(520)329-0990

Central Arizona Association of Governments
230 Main St.
Superior, AZ 85273
(520)689-9044

Central Arizona Association of Governments
414B N. Marshall
Casa Grande, AZ 85222
(520)836-1887

Northern Arizona Re-Employment and Pre-Layoff Assistance Center
100 S. Broad St.
Globe, AZ 85502
(520)425-7631

Graham One-Stop Career Center
1938 W. Thatcher Blvd.
Safford, AZ 85546
(520)428-7079

Greenlee One-Stop Career Center
Hwy 191 and Ward Canyon Rd.
Clifton, AZ 85533
(520)865-4151

Career Redevelopment Center
1145 E. Washington St.
Phoenix, AZ 85034
(602)534-3922

Maricopa Workforce Development Center
5730 W. Hayward, Ste. 63-64
Glendale, AZ 85301
(623)934-3231

Maricopa Workforce Development Center
1300 S. Litchfield Rd. Bldg. 11
Goodyear, AZ 85338
(623)925-0466

Maricopa Workforce Development Center
305 E. Main St. Ste. 200
Mesa, AZ 85201
(480)464-9669

Vista Del Camino Center
7700 E. Roosevelt St.
Scottsdale, AZ 85257
(480)312-2323

West Phoenix Human Service Center
3454 N. 51st Ave.
Phoenix, AZ 85031
(602)262-6510

Kino Teen Center
2801 E. Ajo Wy.
Tucson, AZ 85713
(520)740-4600

Jackson Employment Center
300 E. 26th St.
Tucson, AZ 85713
(520)882-5500

One-Stop Center
1039 N. Stone Ave.
Tucson, AZ 85705
(520)770-9508

Regional Re-Employment Center
2224 N. Craycroft Rd. Ste. 101
Tucson, AZ 85712
(520)290-0923

Regional Re-Employment Center
667 N. 7th Ave.
Tucson, AZ 85705
(520)629-0450

Appendix B

MAJOR EMPLOYERS

This includes companies with 2,000 or more employees. The employer is listed by the name by which it is commonly known in the community. Where possible the numbers listed are for the company's Jobline or the Human Resources Department.

Call first. Many companies discourage drop-in applicants and others have specific requirements for electronic resume submission.

Some employers with a strong presence in Arizona are not listed such as Dillards, Mervyn's, Target, Home Depot and Circle K. Check with a store near you to obtain employment information. Many retailers recruit only at the store level.

Employers may have additional locations, besides the one listed here. Many of these companies also maintain sites on the Internet. Use your search engine to locate these sites.

Employer	Main Arizona Location	Contact	Activity
Albertson's	Tolleson	(800)841-6371	Grocer
Allied Signal	Phoenix	(888)211-5041	Aircraft Engines
America West	Tempe	(480)693-8650	Airline
American Express	Phoenix	(623)492-5627	Travel, Finance
Amphitheater Public Schools	Tucson	(520)696-5021	Public Schools
APS	Phoenix	(602)250-3369	Utility
Arizona State University	Tempe	(480)965-5627	Higher Education
ASARCO	Tucson	(520)648-2500	Mining
Bank of America	Phoenix	(602)416-0678	Banking
Bank One	Phoenix	(800)344-5627	Banking
Bashas	Chandler	(480)895-5229	Grocer
BHP Copper	San Manuel	(520)385-3467	Mining, Smelting
Boeing	Mesa	(480)891-3100	Aircraft
Carondolet Health Network	Tucson	(520)721-3874	Health Care
City of Phoenix	Phoenix	(602)534-5627	Municipality
City of Tucson	Tucson	(520)791-5068	Municipality
Columbia/HCA Healthcare	Phoenix	(602)867-5627	Health Care
Davis-Monthan	Tucson	(520)228-4103	Air Force Base
Fry's Food	Phoenix	(602)352-5326	Grocer
Ft. Huachuca	Ft. Huachuca	(520)533-2468	US Army Base
Honeywell	Phoenix	honeywell.com	Electronics, Aviation

Employer	Main Arizona Location	Contact	Activity
Intel	Chandler	(480)554-8080	Semiconductors
Kyrene Elementary Schools	Tempe	(480)783-4018	Public Schools
Luke Air Force Base	Luke AFB	(623)856-7745	Air Force Base
Maricopa Community Colleges	Tempe	(480)731-8444	Higher Education
Maricopa County	Phoenix	(602)506-3329	Government
Marriot/Host	Phoenix	(888)462-7746	Hotels, Food Service
Mesa Public Schools	Mesa	(480)472-7200	Public Schools
Motorola	Scottsdale	(480)303-6000	Electronics,
Aviation, Computers			
Phelps Dodge	Phoenix	(602)234-8281	Mining, Manufacturing
Pima Community College	Tucson	(520)206-4623	Higher Education
Pima County	Tucson	(520)740-3530	Government
Raytheon Systems	Tucson	(520)794-3000	Missile Systems
Safeway	Phoenix	(480)894-4138	Grocer
Scottsdale Unified Schools	Scottsdale	(602)952-6296	Public Schools
Smith's Food and Drug Centers	Tolleson	(623)936-2400	Grocer
Southwest Airlines	Phoenix	(602)389-3738	Airline
SRP	Tempe	(602)236-8734	Utility
State of Arizona	Phoenix	(602)542-4966	Government

Employer	Main Arizona Location	Contact	Activity
Sunnyside Schools	Tucson	(520)545-2005	Public Schools
TMC Healthcare	Tucson	(520)324-2600	Health Care
TRW Safety Systems	Mesa	trw.com	Air Bags
Tucson Unified Schools	Tucson	(520)617-7216	Public Schools
University of Arizona	Tucson	(520)621-3087	Higher Education
UPS	Phoenix	(888)967-5877	Delivery
US West	Phoenix	(800)678-5627	Telephone, Telecommunications
USPS	Phoenix	(602)223-3624	Postal Service
Wells Fargo	Phoenix	(602)378-1530	Banking

Appendix C

REGULATED OCCUPATIONS

Obtaining a license to work in certain occupations is an important part of preparation for employment. In Arizona, many occupations require licenses. Since no central authority is established within the state, most licensing boards operate autonomously—establishing occupational entry standards, administering examinations (in some cases), and issuing licenses. The following list should help you get started, but it should not be considered comprehensive. Other occupations may be subject to oversight by either state, federal, county or local regulations. Like many other Arizona offices, government offices move frequently. If your agency has outgrown its space it may have a new number. Try the state's general information operator if you have difficulty reaching an office (602) 542-4900.

OCCUPATION	REGULATORY AGENCY
Adoption Agency	Adult Child Youth Family Services (602)542-3981
Adoption Search Intermediary	Dependent Children's Division, Supreme Court (602)542-9410
Adult Care Home Manager	Board of Examiners, Nursing and Adult Care (602)542-3095
Aesthetician, Instructor	Board of Cosmetology (480)784-4539
Aircraft Owner, Dealer	Department of Transportation (602)712-7011
Ambulance Service	Office of Emergency Medical Services (602)861-0708
Appraisal Real and Personal Property	Property Valuation and Equalization Division, Department of Revenue (602)542-3529
Architect	Board of Technical Registration (602)364-4930
Assayer	Board of Technical Registration (602)364-4930
Attorney	State Bar (602)252-4804
Bail Bond Agent	Department of Insurance (602)912-8400

OCCUPATION   REGULATORY AGENCY

Bait Sales
Game and Fish Department
(602)942-3000

Barber
Board of Barbers
(602)542-4498

Bedding Manufacture,   Food and Safety Environmental
Renovation, and Sanitization Services Section
(520)774-5538

Behavioral Health Agency
Department of Health Services
(602)542-1025

Bingo Operation
Bingo Section, Department of Revenue
(602)542-4765

Boat License Sales
Game and Fish Department
(602)942-3000

Boxer and Boxing-related
Boxing Commission
Work
(602)364-1727

Campground Membership
Department of Real Estate
Broker, Sales
(602)468-1414 x100

Cemetery Broker, Sales
Department of Real Estate
(602)468-1414 x100

Certified Public Accountant Board of Accountancy
(602)364-0804

Charitable Solicitor
Secretary of State
(602)542-4285

Child Care Facility, Day
Department of Health Services
Care Group Home
(602)542-1025

OCCUPATION	REGULATORY AGENCY
Child Placement Agency, Residential and Shelter Care	Department of Economic Security (602)542-4761
Children's Camp	Food and Safety Environmental Services Section (520)774-5538
Collection Agency	Banking Department (602)255-4421
Contractor	Registrar of Contractors (602)542-1525
Corporation, Domestic, Foreign, Limited Liability	Corporation Commission (602)542-3135
Cosmetologist, Instructor, Salon	Board of Cosmetology (480)784-4539
Counselor	Board of Behavioral Health Examiners (602)542-1882
Defensive Driving School, Instructor	Defensive Driving Program, Supreme Court (602)364-0388
Dentist, Assistant, Hygienist,Technologist	Board of Dental Examiners (602)242-1492
Doctor of Chiropractic	Board of Chiropractic Examiners (602)864-5088
Dog Racing Kennel	Department of Racing (602)364-1700
Drilling, Water	Department of Water Resources (602)417-2400

OCCUPATION   REGULATORY AGENCY

Drilling-Oil, Gas, Helium etc. Geological Survey
(520)770-3500

Driver Training School,   Department of Transportation
Instructor   (602)712-7011

Drug Wholesaler,   Board of Pharmacy
Manufacturer, OTC Sales   (602)463-2727

DUI Screening, Education,   Department of Health Services
Treatment   (602)542-1025

DUI Test Administration,   Division of State Laboratory Services
Analysis   (602)255-3454

Educational Administrator   Department of Education
(602)542-5393

Educational Supervisor   Department of Education
(602)542-5393

EMT, Instructor   Office of Emergency Medical Services
(602)861-0708

Engineer   Board of Technical Registration
(602)364-4930

Environmental Laboratory   Division of State Laboratory Services
(602)255-3454

Escrow Agent   Banking Department
(602)255-4421

Family Child Care Home   Child Care Administration
(602)542-4248

OCCUPATION	REGULATORY AGENCY
Feedlot Operator	Animal Services Division, Department of Agriculture (602)542-0872
Fiduciary Agent	Banking Department (602)255-4421
Financial Planner	Securities Division of the Corporation Commission (602)542-4242
Food Establishment	Food and Safety Environmental Services Section (602)230-5912
Food or Beverage Handler	County Health Department (local)
Foster Home	Department of Economic Security (602)542-2287
Fruit or Vegetable Broker, Dealer, Packer, Shipper	Fruit and Vegetable Standardization, Department of Agriculture (602)542-9047
Funeral Director, Embalmer	Board of Embalmers (602)542-3095
Funeral Sales (Pre-arranged)	Board of Embalmers (602)542-3095
Fur Dealer	Game and Fish Department (602)942-3000
Game Farms	Game and Fish Department (602)942-3000

OCCUPATION   REGULATORY AGENCY

Geologist   Board of Technical Registration
                                 (602)364-4930

Guide for Big or Small Game Game and Fish Department
                                 (602)942-3000

Hay Dealer   Plant Services Division, Department of
                                 Agriculture
                                 (602)542-0994

Health Screening Service   Division of State Laboratory Services
                                 (602)255-3454

Hearing Aid Dispensers   Office of Health Care Licensure
                                 (602)674-4340

Homeopathic Physician   Board of Homeopathic Medical
                                 Examiners
                                 (602)542-3095

Horse Trader   Animal Services Division, Department of
                                 Agriculture
                                 (602)542-7011

Human Specimen Testing   Division of State Laboratory Services
                                 (602)364-0720

Hunting and Fishing   Game and Fish Department
License Sales   (602)942-3000

Insurance Agent, Broker,   Department of Insurance
Adjuster   (602)912-8470

Investment Adviser   Securities Division of the Corporation
                                 Commission
                                 (602)542-4242

OCCUPATION	REGULATORY AGENCY
Land Surveyor	Board of Technical Registration (602)364-4930
Landscape Architect	Board of Technical Registration (602)364-4930
Lender	Banking Department (602)255-4421
Limited Partnership	Secretary of State (602)542-4285
Liquor Production, Distribution or Sales	Department of Liquor License and Control (602)542-5141
Lobbyist	Secretary of State (602)542-4285
Lottery Sales	Lottery (480)921-4400
Mammography Technologist	Medical Radiologic Technology Board of Examiners (602)255-4845
Manufactured Home (most related services)	Department of Building and Fire Safety, (602)364-1003
Marriage and Family Therapist	Board of Behavioral Health Examiners (602)542-1882
Meat and Poultry Processor	Animal Services Division, Department of Agriculture (602)542-0872

OCCUPATION

REGULATORY AGENCY

Medical Doctor, Intern, Resident	Board of Medical Examiners (480)551-2791
Medical Gas Distributor, Supplier	Board of Pharmacy (602)463-2727
Milk Producer	Animal Services Division, Department of Agriculture (602)542-4189
Mine Operations	Mine Inspector (602)542-5971
Money Transmitter	Banking Department (602)255-4421
Mortgage Banker, Broker	Banking Department (602)255-4421
Motor Carriers	Department of Transportation (602)712-7011
Motor Vehicle Dealer, Broker, Auction Dealer	Department of Transportation (602)712-7011
Nail Technician, Instructor	Board of Cosmetology (480)784-4539
Naturopathic Physician, Specialist, Assistant, Student, School	Board of Naturopathic Physicians Examiners (602)542-8242
Notary	Secretary of State (602)542-4285
Nurse Practitioners	Board of Nursing (602)331-8111

OCCUPATION	REGULATORY AGENCY
Nurses, Practical, Registered, Aids	Board of Nursing (602)331-8111
Nursing Care Administrator	Board of Examiners, Nursing and Adult Care (602)542-3095
Nursing Care Facility	Office of Health Care Licensure (602)674-9705
Off Track Betting Facility	Department of Racing (602)364-1700
Optician, Optical Establishment	Board of Dispensing Opticians (602)542-8164
Optometrist	Board of Optometry (602)542-3095
Osteopathic Physician and Surgeon	Board of Osteopathic Medicine and Surgery Examiners (480)657-7703
Paramedic	Office of Emergency Medical Services (602)861-0708
Pest Control–Structural	Structural Pest Control Commission (602)255-3664
Pesticide, Sales, User	Environmental Services Division, Department of Agriculture (602)542-0949
Pharmacist, Interns, Pharmacy	Board of Pharmacy (602)463-2727

OCCUPATION   REGULATORY AGENCY

Physical Therapist   Board of Physical Therapy Examiners
                                (602)542-3095

Physicians Assistants   Joint Board on the Regulation of
                                Physicians Assistants
                                (480)551-2791

Pilot, Agricultural   Environmental Services Division,
                                Department of Agriculture
                                (602)542-0814

Podiatrist   Board of Examiners
                                (602)542-3095

Podiatry Technologist   Medical Radiologic Technology Board of
                                Examiners
                                (602)255-4845

Pre-School Facility   Department of Health Services
                                (602)674-4300

Process Server   Court Services Division, Supreme Court
                                (602)542-9300

Produce Packer, Shipper   Fruit and Vegetable Standardization,
                                Department of Agriculture
                                (602)542-4373

Property Tax Agent   Board of Appraisal
                                (602)542-1539

Psychologist   Board of Psychologist Examiners
                                (602)542-8162

Racing (most related work) Department of Racing
                                (602)364-1700

OCCUPATION   REGULATORY AGENCY

Radiology Technologist   Medical Radiologic Technology Board of
                                 Examiners
                                 (602)255-4845

Real Estate Appraiser   Board of Appraisal
                                 (602)542-1539

Real Estate Broker, Sales,   Department of Real Estate
Schools, Instructors   (602)468-1414 x100

Respiratory Care   Board of Respiratory Care Examiners
                                 (602)542-5995

Risk Management   Department of Insurance
Consultant   (602)912-8400

Securities Dealer, Sales   Securities Division of the Corporation
                                 Commission
                                 (602)542-4242

Seed Sales   Plant Services Division, Department of
                                 Agriculture
                                 (602)542-0814

Shooting Preserve   Game and Fish Department
                                 (602)942-3000

Social Worker   Board of Behavioral Health Examiners
                                 (602)542-1882

Substance Abuse Counselor   Board of Behavioral Health Examiners
                                 (602)542-1882

Taxidermist   Game and Fish Department
                                 (602)942-3000

OCCUPATION

REGULATORY AGENCY

Teacher, Elementary and Secondary	Department of Education (602)542-5393
Telemarketer	Secretary of State (602)542-4285
Tobacco Sales, Distribution, Vending	Department of Revenue (602)542-4576
Trapper	Game and Fish Department (602)942-3000
Vehicle Emission Inspector	Department of Environmental Quality (602)771-2300
Veterinarian, Technician, Facility	Veterinary Medical Examining Board (602)364-1738
Vocational School	Board of Private Post Secondary Education (602)542-5709
Water Development (most types)	Department of Water Resources (602)417-2400
Weights and Measurements	Department of Weights and Measures (602)255-5211

Appendix D

CHAMBERS OF COMMERCE

Alpine
P.O. Box 410
Alpine, AZ 85920
(520)339-4330

Apache Junction
P.O. Box 1747
Apache Junction, AZ 85217
(480)982-3141

Arizona City
P.O. Box 5
13540 Sunland Gin Rd. Ste. 105
Arizona City, AZ 85223
(520)466-5141

**Avondale/Goodyear/
Litchfield Park
Southwest Valley**
289 Litchfield Park Rd.
Goodyear, AZ 85323
(623)932-2260

Benson
P.O. Box 2223
Benson, AZ 85602
(520)586-2245

Bisbee
Drawer BA
Bisbee AZ 85603
(520)432-5421

Black Canyon City
P.O. Box 1919
Black Canyon City, AZ 85603
(520)374-9797

Bullhead City
1251 Highway 95
Bullhead City, AZ 86429
(520)754-4121

Camp Verde
P.O. Box 3520
Camp Verde AZ 86322
(520)567-9294

Carefree/Cave Creek
P.O. Box 734
Carefree, AZ 85377
(480)488-3381

Casa Grande
P.O. Box 10062
Casa Grande, AZ 85230
(520)836-2125

Chandler
218 N. Arizona Ave.
Chandler, AZ 85224
(480)963-4571

Coolidge
P.O. Box 1498
Coolidge, AZ 85228
(520)723-3009

Douglas
1125 Pan American
Douglas, AZ 85607
(520)364-2477

Flagstaff
101 W. Route 66
Flagstaff, AZ 86001
(520)774-4505

Florence
P.O. Box 929
Florence, AZ 85232
(520)868-9433

Fountain Hills
P.O. Box 17598
Fountain Hills, AZ 85269
(480)837-1654

Gila Bend
P.O. Box CC
Gila Bend, AZ 85337
(520)683-2002

Gilbert
P.O. Box 527
Gilbert, AZ 85234
(480) 892-0056

Glendale
P.O. Box 249
Glendale, AZ 85311
(623)937-4754

Globe/Miami
P.O. Box 2539
Globe, AZ 85502
(520)425-4495

Grand Canyon/Williams
P.O. Box 3007
Grand Canyon, AZ 86023
(520)638-2901

Green Valley
P.O. Box 566
Green Valley, AZ 85622
(520) 625-7575

Heber/Overgaard
P.O. Box 550
Heber, AZ 85928
(520)535-4406

Holbrook
100 E. AZ St.
Holbrook, AZ 86025
(520)524-6558

Jerome
P.O. Drawer K
Jerome, AZ 86331
(520)634-2900

Kingman
P.O. Box 1150
Kingman, AZ 86402
(520)753-6106

Lake Havasu City
314 London Bridge Rd.
Lake Havasu City, AZ 86403
(520)453-3444

Mesa
P.O. Box 5820
Mesa, AZ 85211
(480)969-1307

Nogales/Santa Cruz
Kino Park
Nogales, AZ 85621
(520)287-3685

Oro Valley
11000 N. La Canada Dr.
Oro Valley, AZ 85737
(520)297-2591

Page/Lake Powell
P.O. Box 727
Page, AZ 86040
(520)645-2741

Parker
1217 California Ave.
Parker, AZ 85344
(520)669-2174

Payson
P.O. Box 1380
Payson, AZ 85541
(520)474-4515

Pearce/Sunsites
P.O. Box 308
Pearce, AZ 85625
(520)826-3535

Peoria
P.O. Box 70
Peoria, AZ 85380
(623)979-3601

Phoenix
201 N. Central Ave. Ste. 2500
Phoenix, AZ 85073
(602)254-5521

Pine/Strawberry
P.O. Box 196
Pine, AZ 85544
(520)476-3547

Pinetop/Lakeside
592 W. White Mountain Blvd.
Lakeside, AZ 85929
(520)367-4290

Prescott
P.O. Box 1147
Prescott, AZ 86302
(520)445-2000

Prescott Valley
8098 E. State Route 69 Ste. B
Prescott Valley, AZ 86314
(520)772-8857

Quartzsite
P.O. Box 85
Quartzsite, AZ 85346
(520)927-5600

Scottsdale
7343 Scottsdale Mall
Scottsdale, AZ 85251
(480)945-8481

Sedona-Oak Creek
P.O. Box 478
Sedona, AZ 86336
(520)204-1123

Show Low
P.O. Box 1083
Show Low, AZ 85902
(520)537-2326

Sierra Vista
21 E Wilcox Dr.
Sierra Vista, AZ 85635
(520)458-6940

Springerville
Round Valley
P.O. Box 31
Springerville, AZ 85938
(520)333-2123

Sun City/Sun City West
Northwest Valley Chamber
12425 W. Bell Rd. Ste.C305
Surprise, AZ 85374
(623)583-0692

Tempe
P.O. Box 28500
Tempe, AZ 85285
(480)967-7891

Tombstone
P.O. Box 995
Tombstone, AZ 85638
(520)457-3929

Tubac
P.O. Box 1866
Tubac, AZ 85646
(520)398-2704

Tucson
P.O. Box 991
Tucson, AZ 85702
(520) 792-2250

Verde Valley
1010 S. Main St.
Cottonwood, AZ 86326
(520)634-7593

Wickenburg
216 N. Frontier St.
Wickenburg, AZ 85390
(520)684-5479

Yuma
377 S. Main St. Ste. 203
Yuma, AZ 85364
(520)782-2567

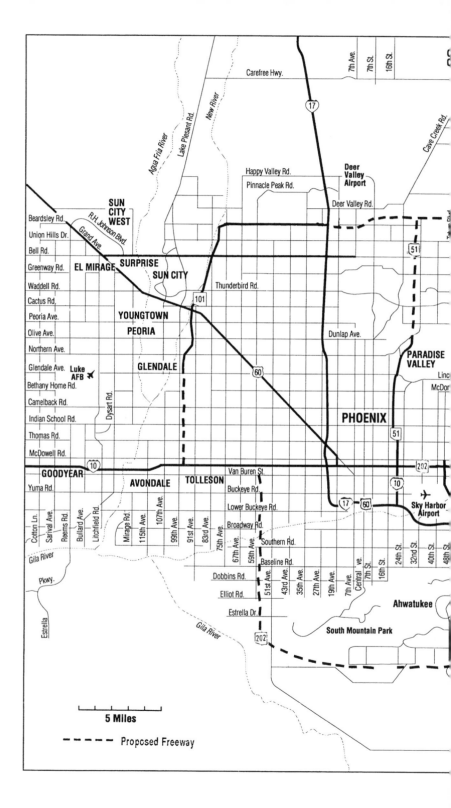

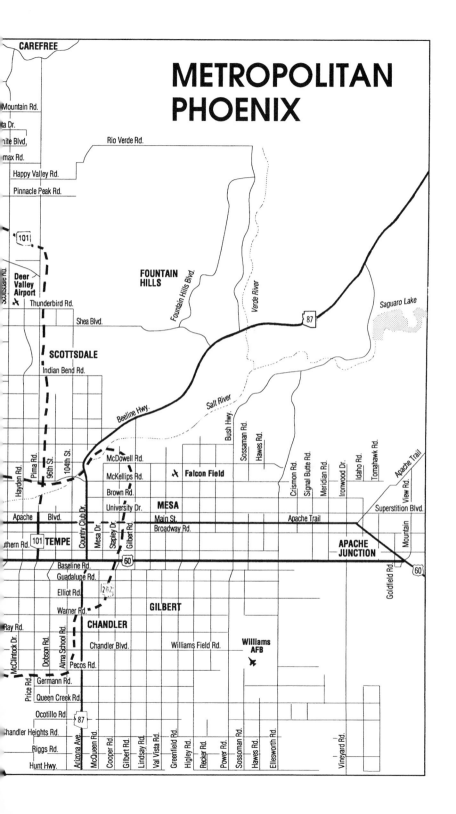

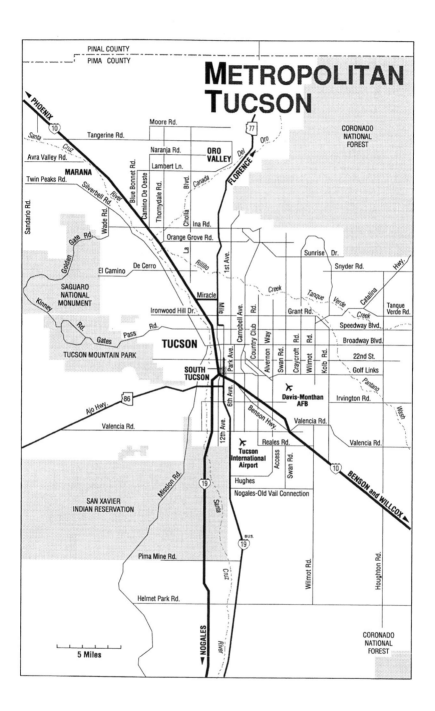

INDEX

ASSORTED TITLES OF INTEREST FOR THE
ARIZONA VISITOR & RESIDENT

BIRDS OF THE SOUTHWESTERN DESERT, Smith. A favorite among bird watchers who observe the desert trails. Fascinating and witty descriptions & color illustrations of desert birds. **$8.95**

DAY HIKES AND TRAIL RIDES IN AND AROUND PHOENIX, Freeman. Revised edition. Topo maps & photos of the many riding & hiking trips within a 40-mile radius of downtown Phoenix. **$14.95**

THE ARIZONA TRIVIA BOOK, Cook. The who, what, when, where of Arizona. Full of interesting and educational facts and trivia. **$6.95**

DRY HUMOR: TALES OF ARIZONA WEATHER, Cook. Humorous look at the folklore and facts behind Arizona's news-making weather. Illustrated. **$6.95**

ARIZONA 101: AN IRREVERENT SHORT COURSE FOR NEW ARRIVALS, Cook. Visitors, newcomers and natives alike will enjoy this irreverent study of Arizona–the language, cowboys and native food. **$7.95**

THE OLD WEST TRIVIA BOOK, Bullis. Page turning questions and historic photos describe everything from the Butterfield Overland Stage Route and Indians of the Southwest to Arizona's colorful characters, gang robbers and cowboys. **$10.95**

GEM TRAILS OF ARIZONA, Mitchell. Revised edition of a bestselling guide covering over 77 collecting sites. Maps, detailed text and photos lead the collector to sites as diverse as the rocks and minerals found there. **$11.95**

GOLD DIGGERS ATLAS, Johnson. This complete book of maps shows where gold has been found in the West and Southwest. **$6.00**

WHERE TO FIND GOLD IN THE DESERT, Klein. Expanded & updated edition of a classic best-seller. Desert gold locations in AZ, CA, and NV with detailed maps and photos. **$7.95**

AVAILABLE AT YOUR LOCAL BOOK STORE, OUTDOOR STORE OR ROCKSHOP.

ABOUT THE AUTHOR

Quoting Arizona facts and figures has become second nature for the *Dorothy Tegeler*. Keeping up with the changes that occur in a busy growing state like Arizona has been challenging. The author's own experiences relocating to Arizona heavily influenced how this book has evolved. Now in its fourth edition, *Moving to Arizona* has become an unofficial Arizona welcome mat.

Like many other visitors to Arizona, the author's first trip to the state more than 18 years ago was love at first sight. Since then she's been immersed in writing about the state. When she's not writing, she's traveling or exploring. She is also involved in counseling, education, and child abuse prevention programs.

She now shares her time between homes in the Phoenix and San Francisco Bay areas.

Additional books available by DOROTHY TEGELER:

DESTINATION PHOENIX
Completely revised guide to the Phoenix area with updated maps and contact information. Includes all the information needed to fully explore the many cultural, historical and recreational sights of interest to tourist and native alike. **$12.95**

RETIRING IN ARIZONA
An indispensable guide for anyone retiring in Arizona. Contains all the latest information contact information on over 40 Arizona communities, detailed housing advice, facts and figures, history and community resources. **$10.95**

HELLO ARIZONA!
Full of puzzles, games, pictures to color and activities that teach kids about Arizona. **$3.50**

NOTES